HOW TO
MULTIPLY YOUR VALUE
& CREATE EXTRAORDINARY IMPACT

HOW TO

MULTIPLY YOUR VALUE

& CREATE EXTRAORDINARY IMPACT

UNOTIDA NYONI

CONTENTS

PRINCIPLES

To Book Unotida Nyoni

www.unonyoni.com

www.facebook.com/unotida.nyoni

www.linkedin.com/unotida-nyoni577b4b27

www.twitter.com/unyoni001

Unotida captures the universal principles of service, leadership and success in this book. I encourage you to read it you are interested in becoming a global change maker.
ArchBishop Desmond Tutu (Emeritus) –Cape Town, South Africa

In this book Unotida share practical and well broken down steps on how one can multiply their value and create a ripple of effect. It is time to step up the game and Unotida has your back in this book - will you bank on yourself and act on the ideas in this book? **Tafadzwa Bete Sasa – Founder of the Goal Getter Movement (Zambia)**

"If you want to increase your influence and impact look no further than this book. I have known Unotida for a long time and he is a practitioner of the personal development and leadership principles he shares in this book. I encourage everyone to buy and read this book."
Simbarashe Nyamadzawo | Author | Speaker | Thought-Leader (Zimbabwe)

This is a superb and highly practical book. Unotida reveals that beyond the clay there is treasure that God has deposited in each one of us. If you are seeking to reveal the treasure within you, then this is your 'one stop book'. I highly recommend it.

Pastor Dan Zimuwandeyi – Senior Pastor of Grace Chapter Church (South Africa)

In this book, Unotida not only highlights the habits of successful business leaders, but also reveals their values and thinking patterns. I recommend it for every aspiring business leader who wants to create sustainable wealth and lasting impact

Luvuyo Rani – Co Founder and Managing Director of Silulo Ulutho Techologies (South Africa)

A must read for every person who wants to positively impact the lives of as many people and make a living while doing it

Erich Schlenker - Managing Director of the Center for Entrepreneurship at Appalachian State University, North Carolina, USA

ACKNOWLEDGEMENTS

First, I want to thank God for giving me the ability to put my thoughts on paper and to share that with the rest of the world. Thank you for reminding me that I have a purpose to give what you have first given to us.

To my wife Ellen Nyoni, thank you for allowing this dream to take shape and to see the light of day. This book was waiting for me to meet you before it could come out into the world. Your presence, support, unwavering faith in my ability and constant encouragement gave me the strength I needed to start the work. Love you babe.

My mom Rev. Enittah Nyoni has always been an inspiration to me. She is the first author in our family, and seeing her teach the principles of her first book "Bitterness" all over the world encouraged me to start on this journey. To my Dad Rev. Lenson Nyoni who has always believed in me and whose story of growth inspires me every day, thank you for nurturing this vision to where it is now.

Along the way, there are people who picked up that I was carrying something that needs to be shared with the world and have encouraged me to go on with it. Mr Givemore Negomo, thank you for always asking the hard questions and encouraging me to follow my calling. Simba Nyamadzawo, my good friend, thank you for everything you shared when you visited. You revived a dormant dream and got me to start. Thank you for introducing me to Rabison Shumba, who ignited the fire even more during our first Success symposium in Cape Town. Mukoma Rabison, thank you for sharing all that you know and passing it on to us.

Precious Muswandigere, thank you for going through the first draft and sharing your encouraging views with me. Faith Marck, your editing work was amazing and I value every point that you spent making changes. To my publishers, the Grayshor team (Mdu and Isaac), thank you for your time, expertise and advice.

In this book, I write about the power of association and self-education. There are a number associations that have helped me get to this stage. Junior Chamber International (JCI) thank you for providing me with the platform for me to identify and practice my purpose as a leader, entrepreneur and active ctizen. The Professional Speakers Association of Southern Africa, thank you for generously sharing information on how to write books and how to run a professional speaking business. Thank you leaders of the Africa Christian Business Fellowship for planting the seeds that made me believe that this could be done. A special shout out to friends in the Mandela Washington Fellowship team too for cheering me on.

To all my former colleagues in the companies that I worked in (Funding Initiatives, PWC Zimbabwe, Silulo Ulutho Technologies and the Desmond and Leah Tutu Legacy Foundation (DLTLF), thank you for the great learning experiences.

To all the pastors who I have worked with, thank you for giving me the platform to share my ideas and develop the gift that God has given me. Pastors Edinger, Gora, Siwela, Rudo Nyoni, Mawarire, Nyambo, Mlilo, Mariga, Zimuwandeyi and the Ndebeles. I appreciate you.

Lastly, I want to thank all the readers of this book. Thank you for making this investment. I know that every time you spend reading any page in this book, you will get to multiply your value and impact in the marketplace.

FOREWORD

One challenge on every living human being's shoulder is to remain relevant to society at large. The only way to leave a lasting legacy and heritage is by ensuring one taps into their inner self to discover what they can contribute to the table of endeavor. The world has enough consumers of what already exists and few contributors of what can be. For some, there is desire and yearning to make a mark, but it ends as just an idea. For others, they start off well and never finish their assignments. This is where I applaud writers like Unotida who are passionate about seeing your potential manifesting. This very book will open your eyes and mind to possibilities that increase your chances of attaining success. It is easy to sit on your potential without realizing that you can indeed multiply your voice, influence and your impact in your own generation. Read this book with a resolve to implement every principle contained herein and not for head knowledge alone. Unotida, well done for stepping out to give us gems to live by. I am thoroughly impressed by your level of wisdom.

Rabison Shumba
Author, Speaker, Business Consultant and Entrepreneur Johannesburg, South Africa.

INTRODUCTION

FROM AS LONG as 13 years ago, I promised myself that I was going to be a student of life. I was going to study, practice, and teach the principles that make individuals, organisations and nations succeed. Having grown up in different parts of Zimbabwe, I began to ask specific questions. I was struck by the level of poverty in my country. As a young man who had attended school in a rural setting as well as an urban setting, I noticed specific differences between the two areas that made me ask the question: "What are these people doing differently to make their life easier and better?"

After high school, I worked as a trainee auditor in one of the big-four accounting firms in the world. I had an opportunity to work with thriving companies and struggling companies, too. As an auditor, I had to interact with the general workers who earned little, and with the CEOs who earned so much. I read about the shareholders and leaders of great companies. In my mind was a burning question. "How come others have it going so well, and yet others seem to be struggling just to survive?"

After completing my articles, I thought the best place to understand my search would be to go and study again, and then work with some thriving entrepreneurs, so that I understand the difference. I had already made this my life's mission – 'To study, practice and teach principles throughout my life.' So I went to do a Masters in Business Administration and studied how big companies made it, how great social entrepreneurs were making things happen, and how great economies in the world could achieve that greatness. In my heart was a deep longing to see the continent of Africa thrive. That deep desire has grown stronger, and that's why I decided to put my observations, experiences, and studies into a book.

We cannot continue to be left behind as the rest of the world progresses. We cannot continue to have our people dying of hunger and poverty. We cannot continue to be the "dark continent", and yes, I have heard some comments about us being the "next frontier," but for goodness sake, that's too low for us. We are endowed with close to a billion people and with the best natural resources in the world, so this suffering must stop!

Here's what I discovered in my search for solutions. I discovered that the African people are the biggest asset that the continent has, and we have the power to make things change. I discovered that no individual positive effort is insignificant in achieving the greater common good. I discovered that it's all up to us. It's all up to me, and it's all up to you. Why us? "Only human beings can re-order their lives any day they choose by refining their philosophy." As individuals, we can change our value, and as we replace that value, we permit others to do the same. There are timeless, universal principles that we can use to change the status that we have.

Through my involvement as a leading member in organisations such as JCI (Junior Chamber International), I developed a certain mindset that made me believe that, indeed, 'earth's greatest treasure lies in human personality.' I worked with many young people who were game-changers in their communities. Some of them were awarded as most outstanding young people in the world, and I had an opportunity to see the change that they were making.

I also got to work with some of the world's biggest global icons, talked to them, and studied what had been written about them. As I did this, I got more and more excited!! These were ordinary people who did extraordinary things and therefore made a massive difference in their communities. These were global shapers, change-makers, who had decided to move away from the norm and do things differently. What excited me the most was that I could see that the rest of us can do the same things too and make our contribution to the world.

Through this book, I have made my observations simple and easy to follow. It is through the sharing of such knowledge that we can emancipate ourselves from where we are.

So let's get to the title of the book, 'Multiplying your value.' Earlier on, in my search for answers, I came across some wise counsel from the books, programs, and articles of the late Jim Rohn. Much of what he wrote and said made me desire to search more. Here are some of his quotes on the question of value in the marketplace.

- "The market does not pay you what you need; it pays you what you deserve."
- "If you want to have more, become more. For things to improve, you have to improve. For things to be better, you have to get better. For things to change, you have to change. When you change, everything changes for you."

- "We can have more than we've got because we can become more than we are."
- "We don't get paid for the hour; we get paid for the value we bring to the hour."
- "We get paid for bringing value to the marketplace. It takes time… but we get paid for the value, not the time."
- "To become financially independent, you must turn part of your income into capital, turn capital into an enterprise, turn enterprise into profit, turn a profit into an investment, and turn the investment into financial independence."

His story of success, and the stories of many more who left us the gifts of their findings in books is what inspired me to continue with this work.

The word "**value**" is defined as "*the regard that something is held to deserve; the **importance**; **worth**, or **usefulness** of something.*" For example, we can take a family-owned property, a two-bedroomed flat in an urban area. Its value can be explained in three different ways.

The first way that one could look at the value of this property to this family is through the memories that they have about it. If it was a gift from their parents, it carries more sentimental value to the owners and thus is **significant** property to them. If this is where most of their kids grew up, it even becomes a thing of great **importance** to them.

The second way is in its **usefulness** to the people that use it as a home. If they were to describe its value, they would say that it is the place they use for shelter, and it allows them to protect themselves from bad weather conditions outside. They use the place to rest, relax, interact, procreate, and the list goes on. That is how **useful** the property is to the family.

The third way they can describe the value is that the property is an investment. When asked to describe its value, they will talk about the market price or the cost, and thus they describe the value according to how much the property is **worth** financially to them.

Using the three ways of defining the value of a property, we can now start talking about how this value works when it comes to people. It may sound weird, but it can be seen in different ways. Our importance as a human race is unquestionable. Our significance as individuals is immeasurable. From the day we were born into this world, we were already an essential gift to the world. Not only were we necessary to the whole world's ecosystem, but we were also crucial to the people around us. We are unique creatures with characteristics and abilities like no other. Ancient scriptures say: *"What is man that thou art mindful of him? You have made him a little lower than the angels, and crowned him with glory and honour."*

Without doing anything at all, you are so valuable, irreplaceable and unique. You are a gift to the world. When you laugh, talk, love, sing, you add light to the world. Some people make others feel less important, or they gain their sense of importance through belittling others. Their understanding is weak, and they only hurt themselves in the process of belittling others.

Being important is one thing; being useful is another. While we have this intrinsic value as a human family, we can decide to be useful or useless human beings. It is in this definition that we begin to differentiate the value that people have. Just as we described the two-bedroomed flat's usefulness to its owners, we can describe our use to fellow human beings and the world. A house is a form of shelter for the family. The man can also become a protector, a shield, a provider and the list goes on.

Now, it is from this usefulness that we also derive marketplace value. Unlike the property that can be sold to another owner, ours is a different form of value. We cannot be sold (as in the days of slavery), but we can decide where we want to be useful and how we want to be rewarded for our usefulness. This is where my focus has been in writing this book. This, I believe, is the key to our breakthrough as a continent. This is where the multiplier comes in. We can decide what we want to be known for, how we can get there, and what value we want to have in the world.

What Is To Multiply?

Now, what is to multiply? Well, there are many definitions, but for this book, this is the definition that we are looking at: "To increase or cause to increase greatly in number or quantity." Some synonyms of multiply are: increase exponentially, grow, become more numerous, accumulate, proliferate, mount up, mushroom, burgeon, spread, and expand. I'm sure you get the idea now.

The question that I am answering in this book is: "How can we increase our value exponentially, such that we can take care of our people, and none of us will die of hunger in our motherland?" Moreover, how can we spread this value to the rest of the world so that we are equal beneficiaries of the gifts that we were given in the world? The more specific question is: "How can you, as an individual, multiply this value?" As an individual, you are a significant part of the "we".

I believe that when we focus on this, we can spread that value and through our different journeys, light up the world and make it a better place. It is you, the individual, that I am interested in focusing on, because I believe that once one of us is enlightened, it is easier to have more people enlightened. Within you is a generation waiting to be born. Some kids and grandchildren will, or have already come out of you. Your philosophy of life (whether good or bad) will inevitably spread out to others. So let's forget about others for now, and deal with you and me, the individuals who carry such a huge responsibility to make the world a better place. Yes, we are in the business of **YOU** in this book.

PART 1 UNDERSTAND YOURSELF

Discover The Platinum Lining In You

I WOKE UP early that morning and made sure I was ready for the auspicious day at work. I could not wait because it was one of the few adventures that we were set to go for as an audit team at PricewaterhouseCoopers Zimbabwe. I walked from my flat to the pick-up point. The streets of Harare were still free from the noise and traffic congestion. I was already waiting at our pick-up point in town by 6:30 am. There I found a fellow trainee auditor who had just arrived and so we started the usual talk. In no time, our manager Simba arrived and picked us up. Two more vehicles were coming with other team members. Our senior Partner Tinashe was also coming for this trip. That just showed me how serious this audit was for the company. We were now on our way to Zimbabwe Platinum Mine – one of our biggest clients at the time.

Our major business of the day was to have a tour of the mine so that we could understand how the business operates. We were excited about this one. At least it wasn't going to be a whole day of sitting and analysing figures as auditors are usually known to be doing. It was my second time on this audit, but I had never really seen everything in terms of the operational part of the business, and so I was excited. In no time, we were on our way to the biggest platinum mine in the country; the second-largest producer in the world.

On arrival at the mine, we got to the boom gates and had to go through security checks. This showed that there was something of value in this place. You wouldn't protect anything that is not of value, right? I couldn't wait to see the whole place. Once we got to one of the sites, one of the chief accountants and some of the leading operation managers at that time welcomed us.

The tour began. I remember hearing so much about the many minerals extracted from this mine. The manager talked about the platinum group metals that were present in high concentration in this part of the country. I remember hearing of these minerals repeatedly during our audits for that year, and in the few more years that I went to the mine. These were Platinum, Osmium, Iridium, Ruthenium, Rhodium and Palladium. *"They have similar physical properties, and they occur together in the same mineral deposits. Each of them has different uses,"* explained the manager.

My manager, Simba then responded with a question. *"Oh, that's great, Mr Muswandigere. Would you mind telling us about some of the uses of these different minerals that are found in this mining operation?"*

He had taken the words right out of my mouth. I was wondering what made the minerals so special that so much money and other resources were invested in producing these metals.

"Most certainly Simba," the manager replied. *"These metals have many useful catalytic properties. They are highly resistant to wear and tarnish, making platinum, in particular, well-suited for fine jewellery. Some of these minerals are used in different industrial applications since*

they have a high resistance to chemical attack, have excellent high-temperature characteristics and stable electrical properties."

For a moment, this manager took me back to school, where we were studying physical science and chemistry. I sucked at these subjects, so all I could do was a nod in agreement, but couldn't wait to get out and continue with this fantastic tour without being taken back to my struggles with these difficult subjects.

Right in the middle of the tour, I started thinking about how important the discovery of these minerals was to my country and to all the people who were now employed at the mine. I started thinking about how many families were being fed because of this operation and how these minerals were creating so much value from the time of extraction up to the time they were processed to final products. It then dawned on me that just next to this mine was a community of impoverished people who stayed in the area.

"Did they know about these minerals?" my mind started wondering. I remember seeing some of them as we were approaching the mines. They were busy farming, using their domestic animals and ploughs to till the land. *"Did the ancestors know about the great dyke and this platinum belt and the uses of the metals under the ground that they were stepping on? Did they know the gift that God had bestowed upon their land and the potential of this land to feed them and the next generations?"* The answer to the question was a resounding *"NO"*. My mind conversation continued. *"If they knew about all this, they would be the owners of this mining operation, surely."* They would have stopped farming and started looking for investors who could help them establish something more valuable to them.

As we were driving back home that day, I couldn't stop the conversation in my mind. It was as if another voice began to speak to me. The voice audibly said to me, "What you saw at that mine is similar to what happens to many people. They have different groups of platinum deposits in them, but they are busy trying to farm, and as a result, they die poor and unfulfilled. If only they could explore and discover what is in them, they would be amazed at how much value they have to offer to so many people around the world."

This is where my search for knowledge began. I made it a point to start exploring the gifts given to human beings; gifts that lie dormant. I told myself that I could never allow myself to die poor due to lack of knowledge about my potential. I wanted to find out how people could discover their potential and find a way to multiply the value of what was already given to them at birth.

In the rest of this book, I will take you through some of the things that I discovered in my research, in my practice and my observations, that could help you discover your platinum lining. Just like the raw platinum group metals are processed to make final products such as jewellery, I will also take you through some of the processes that you can use to transform your raw talents into something worth much more than you can imagine. Generations to come can benefit from this journey of discovery, so why not take it with me?

Knowing Your SHAPE

Each of us have a unique design and purpose in life. It is our duty to find, understand, and pursue it with all that we have. Imagine this: There are several hundred dollar bills on the floor. You see them in the toilet rolled around a hard, round-shaped paper, usually used for the soft toilet paper. Whoever put them there wants you to use them as toilet paper. That is an example of what could happen if we do not understand our purpose and design. Instead of being in the banks and shops, facilitating trade, the 100-dollar bills are being placed in a wrong room where they are least needed. Their best value is in the wallet and the marketplace. Now imagine that the opposite also takes place, where the toilet paper is being given out in the banks to facilitate trade. The market would be confused. Some of us are in that place of confusion. We have not studied our SHAPE and therefore are placed in wrong places and are doing things that we are not best placed for. We need to find that unique design and purpose so that we may pursue it and fulfil our mission.

Many books have been written about purpose, and I would recommend that you find and read them further. In all my studies of this subject, one description that helped me understand this was from a book called the **'Purpose Driven Life'** by Dr Rick Warren. There is a section in that book entitled **'Understanding your SHAPE'**. I want to use the acronym from that book to explain and simplify the issue of purpose. I will use easy examples and give suggestions on how you, too, can use this tool/framework to understand your place and purpose in life. This acronym is also important to me because I used it in my first international speaking engagement in 2009 in Yamoussoukro, Cote D'Ivoire at the JCI Africa & Middle

East conference during the public speaking competitions. I came out as the winner of those competitions, and I guess that's why the acronym has stuck with me since that time. I always refer to this model in my thinking and processing of where I would like to go in life. I have changed it a bit too, so that it can be used in the broader sense of finding purpose and focusing on what we are best placed for.

The acronym SHAPE stands for:
- **S**pirit of a winner
- **H**eart
- **A**bilities
- **P**ersonality
- **E**xperiences

Now, let's go down the description of each of the above aspects as it relates to our lives.

SHAPE – Embracing The Spirit Of A Winner Within You

Within you lies a giant, a fighter and survivor who has made it up to this day. The fact that you are reading this book means that you have managed to overcome so many battles in life. One obvious battle that you have fought is that of illiteracy. You had to go through schooling, and you gained a remarkable skill that many people are struggling to acquire. That skill is an asset that will take you places.

The other important thing is that you are alive today. Death could have taken you, and there are many chances that sickness could have held you down and you would be in the grave, but here you are today, having fought all opposition to your life, consciously or unconsciously. That should tell you that there is something of a winning nature within you.

One of my mentors used to repeat to us at each point, that we are winners by nature. As we sat down to listen to him, he would repeat to us: *"Did you know that when you were formed at reproduction, more than a billion sperms were fighting to get to the egg? And it is the sperm that represented a part of you that made it first. A different sperm could have produced someone different, but here you are today."*

We take many of these things for granted, and forget to be grateful that we are experiencing life, health, and happiness most of the time. Yet recognising these simple but powerful truths can help us realise that we have more than we think and can do more than we have credited ourselves.

You may not have contributed significantly to who you have now become, but there is evidence that you have conquered many obstacles for you to be here. Some of the battles, you did not fight. Perhaps your parents fought for you, and some were just mere luck or good fortune when you think about it. That is evidence enough to convince you that you have a purpose for being alive and there is something special you are supposed to contribute to this world. You have the spirit of a winner.

Let's stop for a moment and get into a simple exercise that will bring awareness of the spirit of a winner that you have always carried from the day you were born. Take a pen and paper and for the next ten minutes, answer the following questions. Write as much as you can. Don't put the pen down until your ten minutes are over. Write as the thoughts come to your head. Here are a few questions that I would like you to answer.

- List five things you are proud of that you've already accomplished in your life.
- What obstacles have you had to overcome for you to accomplish these things?
- What other obstacles/problems have you had to overcome for you to be alive today?

As we honestly answer these questions, we realise that we are lucky people. We are more than lucky; we are fortunate and profoundly blessed. We have the spirit of winning within our nature. We must always remind ourselves no matter what happens, that we are winners by nature. We have the spirit of winners. This positive mental attitude is one big weapon we need to realise and accomplish our purpose.

As a Christian, the above facts lead me to a more profound conclusion supported in ancient scripture. That conclusion, as I have come to find out, is also the same conclusion that many other religions have reached as well. The conclusion is this: **"God eternally and unconditionally loves us."** Now, that right there is great news, my friends. Knowing this fact alone and personalising it will change the way you walk, talk and even treat yourself. God is the only one with the ability to give the kind of love that surpasses all our understanding and earthly norms. This love is eternal. That means it is not affected by time. He loved us before we were formed in our mother's wombs, He loves us now, and He will love us forever. Our parents, brothers, sisters, neighbours and the rest of the community may come short when they try to give us this kind of love, but God will never come short, not at any time.

His love for us is also unconditional. When we love, it's always because we have admired something about people and it usually comes with conditions of loyalty, obedience, and the likes. Not so with God. He is the only one who will love us regardless of what we do or what we fail to do. An ancient scripture says that "He understands that we are dust", which means He understands and embraces our humanity. A deeper understanding of this conclusion will always lead to a more peaceful, meaningful, and productive life. It will break the hold of stress, fear, and condemnation and will release a fulfilled life that impacts the world. I know that some people will find this hard to swallow because they do not believe in the existence of God or a Higher Power. My message to you is that God's love surpasses and goes beyond our unbelief. We don't need to believe that He is there for this conclusion to be true, so we are all covered by His love.

As we conclude on the "S", I encourage you to take this personal exercise of repeating this statement to yourself at any point that you choose. **"I am eternally and unconditionally loved by God."** This will unleash the spirit of a winner in you to fulfil your purpose.

Until it sinks into your mind that you are special, designed for a purpose, and have a unique contribution to make, you will always live below your God-given potential. Your subconscious mind must know that you are a winner by nature.

I was listening to a recording by Dr Myles Munroe, and something struck me about what he said. He argued that we should have the attitude of a lion in the animal kingdom. He supported that by explaining how the lion was not the fastest, biggest or smartest animal in the jungle, but was the most feared/respected animal. On the other hand, the elephant, in spite of its size, is extremely afraid of the lion. Although the elephant's size could work to its advantage in terms of protecting it from the lion, it finds itself in constant fear of the lion. When the lion sees an elephant, he thinks one word - "lunch". He acts the way he thinks. He attacks because he thinks he can eat the elephant. When the elephant sees a lion, he thinks one word - "eater". He starts retreating or running away with fear of being eaten. Both animals obey their instinctive thoughts. The difference in their attitude about what they see determines their level of respect in the animal kingdom. Allow me to take that example to extract some lessons about value.

1. If you do not believe in your value or worth as a person, you will be undervalued in the marketplace despite the talents, abilities and solutions that you have. Nothing else will function at the level that will give you fulfilment. You will keep searching for your worth in every other place such as in education, relationships, friendships, and even in your job. That external focus as you search for worth can make you end up in abusive situations such as joining gangsters, drug abuse, prostitution and the list goes on. The lack of self-worth will also attract abusive people who know how to manipulate the void that you have. They will use you to their advantage as they give you a false sense of worth that destroys the potential value that you have.

A gifted potential entrepreneur will stay in employment for the rest of his life, as long as his belief system does not allow him to think of taking a leap and trying new things. Now that I have talked about entrepreneurship, let me tell you a story about what I noticed about entrepreneurship cultures in different parts of the world.

Ellen (my wife) and I visited some friends in Bangalore, India, ahead of a JCI world congress that was taking place in Goa. The visit was part of our first anniversary celebration, and so we were super excited to be visiting that country for the first time. As with many of my trips, I take time to study the practices and culture of different people. I usually want to look at what makes certain people thrive in any area of interest. As my wife and I were enjoying this visit and being taken to areas in that state, I made it a point that I would let the JCI national president of India know that I was in his country and would love to meet with some members in the area. A few hours later, I received a call from the chapter president of JCI Bangalore Garden City saying that they would love to see us and get to know us. We went for a light dinner with about ten of their board members and joined their Annual General Election meeting the next day. What stood out for me during that visit was that almost all the members of this chapter owned their companies. The few that were employed full-time had a company that they were working with on the side.

Having been in JCI for a long time and being a numbers man, I could see a striking difference in the percentage uptake of full-time entrepreneurship as a career path compared to my country and even my continent. I asked them why this is so. The answers that I received from my Asian brothers were thought-provoking. It was a part of their upbringing and culture that they would be more inclined to this route than being employed. Some had their business ventures passed on to them by their parents, and for some, these were new ventures that they had started using the lessons they had learnt from their parents or relatives' family businesses. As we travelled the streets of Bangalore, I could easily see that this was an emerging market economy with some different air in its atmosphere. The people at all levels seemed naturally enterprising, even in the smallest of ways.

Interestingly too, my JCI friends were as equally intrigued by the observation that many of their African friends were usually full-time employees in big companies in their home countries. I could now see how this was playing out. In most African, South American, and Caribbean countries, the practice of taking the entrepreneurship route is not as high as it is in Asia, the US, and Europe. As you talk to the people from these areas, you can see the difference in the upbringing and culture. I therefore concluded that there are many entrepreneurs in Africa who should step out of their comfort zone.

2. We are a product of our beliefs. The value that we have in the marketplace has its foundation in our beliefs. No one can live beyond the limits of their belief. The elephant will not suddenly find itself fearlessly attacking the lion using its size and trunk to its advantage. The thought of even trying that will not come through.

   On the other hand, the lion will always find itself in attack mode, using its jaws, speed and roar to its advantage, even if it seems dangerous to do so. It instinctively believes that its lunch is with that elephant and will take the risk of attacking an animal that's bigger and stronger than it is. Can you see how their belief systems determine the actions of these two different animals? When your belief system is self-limiting, there are things that you will never try. You will not even think of trying those things. Let me add a bit of my personal story to this. My first swimming experience was when I was ten years old.

My dad had decided to move us to a more developed school with a swimming pool. Having spent the first ten years of my life in a rural area in Mberengwa in Zimbabwe, this privilege had not come my way. I remember being excited after my mom bought me these awesome looking pair of swimming trunks. I couldn't wait to take my first dive. So when it was time for our class to go for our swimming lesson, I was super excited. I never told anyone that I couldn't swim. So when the time came for my group to take our first swim, I remember just diving into the pool like I knew what I was doing. Boy was I about to learn a lesson☺. First of all, I did not dive in. I fell into the water, tummy first. Secondly, I remember struggling with my movements in the water and sinking at the same time. Someone had to come and get me out because this was just about to become an emergency. The embarrassment that came with having to explain that I could not swim but was trying my luck was intense. As a result, I started hating the swimming class. I would try to avoid it by all means. However, I do remember learning how to float a little bit and walking in the shallow end of the pool several times, but I never really got the hang of swimming.

After that, I now had a belief in my head that swimming was not for me. Even way after that, I never tried swimming, though many opportunities were afforded to me in other schools that I attended. Fast forward to a few months ago. My wife and I bought an apartment in a big, lovely complex in Cape Town. Our flat is overlooking that pol area. In fact, from our bedroom, we could see all the people getting into the pool area and having fun. However, given my primary school experience, I never thought about us using that pool, although it's something that we should be enjoying. It took a couple of friends of ours who insisted that they wanted to come and swim with us for us to agree to take a swim.

After twenty-four years of avoiding swimming, I was pleasantly surprised to find out that I could not only float like I used to, but I could now swim. My friends and wife were looking at me, and I looked like a natural swimmer. I now have the excitement of a little kid. I go to the pool at least twice a week to enjoy the swim. This got me thinking. If I had continued practising a little bit more twenty-four years ago, I would have realised that I gave up too early, and I would have enjoyed swimming all this time. The beach would not have been as scary as it was for me. Who knows, it could have been a great sport for me in school. However, I had convinced myself that swimming was not for me. It was a self-limiting belief that made me lose out on something that I now enjoy.

In the same way, there are many things that we could be missing out on in life because our belief system tells us not to try. What if we are naturals in those areas? Food for thought, right?

SHAPE – Paying Attention To The Heart

The heart represents the combination of desires, dreams, interests, hopes, ambitions and affections that you have. We may all grow up in the same family and live in the same place, but we have differences when it comes to what our hearts want. I come from a family of five kids, raised by the same parents, went to the same schools and same church, but I could tell you stories about each one of us and how we are different in what we are passionate about. The passions may be in the same area but may have various forms of expression, and that shows how different we are as far as our hearts are concerned.

There are many things that my parents and siblings could have wanted me to do and even pursue as a career, that I just felt were not in my area of passion. The same applies to them. If there is one thing that I have learnt about my siblings and parents, it is that we are different and so are our hearts. There are times I have attempted to change and push some of them into loving the same things that I love, but the more I would do that, the more we would grow apart because they have different sets of desires, dreams, interests, hopes and ambitions. I realised that all I have to do is to appreciate and understand them for who they are. The best way to show that I love them is to help them accomplish their own heart's desires. When I started doing this, we became close once again. Many times, I have also tried to fit in and become like some of them, and I found out that the more I did so, the more I lost my sense of happiness and joy. However, when I begin paying attention to my own heart and pursuing my desires, I become free and genuinely happy.

Are you paying attention to your own heart? As you plan your career, business, marriage, spiritual life, physical and mental wellness, are you considering what your heart wants? Studies have shown that people excel the most in areas of their passion. Most successful entrepreneurs were extremely passionate about their area of business before the thought of making money came into their minds. It is their passion that carried them through the difficult times in their businesses, when breaking even was still a dream, and when they went through legal battles and faced numerous obstacles. This does not only apply to individuals but organisations as well. Studies have shown that organisations that do well over an extended time shared a similar passion. That's what held them together and made them focus on a particular dream. We mustn't fight to pursue what other people want us to pursue, but what we already have in our hearts.

Now let's talk about ambition for a moment. Of all the attributes of the heart, I believe that ambition is the critical driver for finding your treasure. Ambition is a strong (earnest; intense) desire for some achievement or distinction (such as power, honour, freedom, association, fame or wealth) and the willingness to strive for its attainment. Ambition is what separates the successful people and organisations from those who do not make it. When the desire is so strong as described above, it gives one a clear mental picture of what the future will be. That mental picture, if given much room to dwell in the mind (conscious & subconscious mind) will drive the actions of the individual or the organisation towards the attainment of the desired goal. Fortunately, ambition is free and easily attainable by all. Unfortunately, not many give it much room to dwell in their minds and make sufficient changes that allow them to achieve the much-desired success.

I admire the work of Trevor Noah, the comedian who is now the host of the Daily Show in the USA. At 32, he had managed to achieve what others could only dream of in their lifetime. His story as told in the book, **'Born A Crime'** shows the poor background from which he came, and it is fascinating to see that he has managed to inspire millions of people across the globe through his comedy. The Daily Show gives him a platform to become more than a comedian. He has become a defender of human rights, a motivational speaker and indeed, an icon in his chosen field. I listened to one of his interviews with DJ Fresh on SA Metro FM's Fresh Breakfast show and was struck by something that he said about ambition. He said that most South Africans are admirably humble people, which makes them unique. However, compared to the American community, which he is now working in, the South African community needs to step up on ambition. As he said that, I gave that statement some thought and realised that it was not just a South African statement. It was an African statement. Could it be that we remain a *"dark continent"* because we are not tapping into this gift of ambition? Could it be that we are not giving ourselves enough room to dream, imagine and fire up the desire within us to take some bold and courageous actions? Are we teaching our children to be ambitious enough? Do we allow them to imagine the possibilities? Do we give ourselves enough room to imagine the possibilities, outside of our ordinary realities?

The book, **'Think & Grow Rich'** by Napoleon Hill is full of great examples of how so many great men achieved greatness through the process of allowing their dreams to take over their minds and eventually take over their actions. It is a great book to read about ambition. All great men who have achieved so much in the world were ambitious people. They had a great mental picture of what was to come, and that is what pulled them through tough times. This goes for all kinds of achievers such as

Martin Luther King Jnr who had a dream of a free society; Christ whose ambition was to free the world from sin and sit at the right hand of The Father; Nelson Mandela's dream of an equal society; and the list goes on and on. We can even look at each of our own lives and see where ambition has taken us. It is time we give ourselves enough freedom and time to DREAM and to be ambitious. We need more people to be well accomplished in the world so that we can create a better place for all. Only those who are ambitious enough can dream of a world of possibilities and get to experience great success as they solve some of the world's biggest problems.

Now, let's get back to your heart. You have dreams that are in you, and because you are so unique and special, your dreams are unique to you. How you visualise your future is going to be different from how I visualise mine. That makes your dreams and ambitions special and valuable. You need to listen to your heart, (your interests, hopes, affections and dreams) and let it express itself tangibly and powerfully. One of the ways that you do that is through writing your dreams down. There is power in writing things down, because we express the thoughts of the mind in a structured way that we can always come back to, to reignite the same dreams. Writing it down gives the thought a place to stay and provides the dream with its first form of physical life. It ceases to remain in the head only, where it can be easily lost or forgotten. It now goes onto a paper where it can be read and brought to life many times. One of my mentors calls this the process of immortalising your thoughts. Even the ancient scriptures took note of the importance of writing. *"Write the vision; make it plain on tablets so he may run he who reads it,"* it says.

Here is an exercise that will take about half an hour, depending on how intense you want it to be. Some call it goal setting. I call it giving my dreams their first form of expression. Take a pen and paper. Go into a quiet place. I usually do it with soft music in the background, so you can allow yourself to do the same if it works for you. The choice of paper is also essential. If you can, use a diary that you will not lose or a book of value that you can refer to for an extended time. If you have a computer, phone or tablet, you can also use that to write, as long as you can store this for a long time. Now here we go:

What do you want in the next ten years? List 50 things at random that you would want to achieve in the next ten years. This can be in any area of your life (social, career, health, economic and personal).

Social can include:
- Relationships
- Giving – How much to whom?
- Family

Career can include:
- Vocation
- Job goals
- Education
- Business goals
- Health can include:
- Mental
- Physical
- Spiritual

Economic can include:
- The state of your finances
- Income & expenses
- Net worth
- Assets & debts
- Retirement savings

Now that you have compiled your list, put your goals into categories of 1, 3, 5 and 10 years. So if you think that a particular goal that you wrote will take place within five years, write a five next to it, if 1, 3 or 10 years, do the same for all items on your list.

- From the list of goals to take place in the next one year, highlight the four most important goals.
- Why are these four goals vital to you? Feel free to write as many reasons as you like for each of the goals.
- Are there any changes that you need to make for you to achieve these goals? Also, write them down.

I would encourage you to go through this process thoroughly and give yourself time with it. There is no need to hurry to finish reading the book if the process of transformation will not take place. It is the transformation that will bring about the positive change that you desire. I have been personally using this structure to my goal setting every year since 2009, and the results have been remarkable. Before that, I had come across many teachings about writing my thoughts and goals down and was practising it all the time.

One event that I remember vividly was when I was sixteen years old, and I was thinking about the career path that I wanted to take. I was writing my Ordinary level exams that year, and as I was busy studying, I thought it would be great to write my dreams down. I wrote that I wanted to pass my exams with distinctions, go to a better school for my Advanced level education. I specifically wrote in that book that I wanted to attain 15 points (3 straight distinctions) for my Advanced level, get a place to do articles and become a chartered accountant. I remember writing exactly why this was important to me and how I prayed to God as I wrote my desires. I am 32 years old now, and all that has happened in my life. More has happened. There is power in writing our desires down. We bring dreams to life, and our minds begin to force us to work to achieve those dreams. I believe there is also a part that God takes care of in the fulfilment of these dreams, but we have to start this process, at least if we are to achieve anything in our lives.

Steve Covey said it in his book, **'The 7 Habits of Highly Effective People'**. He says everything is created twice. It is a vision first and then it is taken into reality. Global organisations and governments have adopted this strategy for many years now. The United Nations used to work with the Millennium Development Goals (MDGs) and is currently working on the Sustainable Development Goals (SDGs). Companies hire strategy consultants to find assistance to come up with their plans. As an individual, challenge yourself to go through your planning processes. This is a great process of activating your faith.

SHAPE – Identifying And Making Use Of Your Abilities

When you combine your passion and ability to meet a great human need, the real magic starts to happen. Abilities are natural talents/gifts that you were born with. Some are gifted with being able to dance, to sing, to talk, to apply the mind in mathematical problems, lead, teach, sell, do well in sports, the list is endless. The key is to recognise the gift, direct it, and apply it in your life for meeting a human need. When we talk about a human need, please note that it goes beyond meeting basic needs such as food, shelter and clothing. You can meet a human need to be entertained, to connect with others, to be seen, heard and recognised, to earn a living, and the list is also endless.

There is an ancient story told about a rich man who had three servants and was going away on a mission. He is said to have left his three servants with several talents, which in those ancient times represented valuable sums of money. He gave each one of them a different number of talents and went away. Upon his return, he asked the three servants how they had used the talents. Two of the servants had used their talents and doubled the amount of money they had. One had hidden his talent and kept it in the ground, and kept it as is. The ancient story has it that the rich man took away the one talent that he had given to the lazy, unproductive servant and gave it to the one who had made five more from what he had.

The great lesson that we must learn from this story is that an ability/talent that is unused or unexercised is as good as lost. Are there any abilities that you are not making use of? Those gifts are as good as gone. You have a lifetime to recognise and use them, but it is up to you to see how you can make more out of those abilities.

My interpretation of making more is merely meeting more human needs. It is serving more people with your abilities and changing their state of affairs because of your intervention or because of your solutions. A great friend of mine once told me that, *"money comes as you solve people's problems, and it multiplies as the number of people you serve grows."* That was profound. He broke down the world of business into a simple statement. The same applies to social entrepreneurs and politicians and in many other aspects of life.

The second great lesson from the ancient story is that it is inevitable for your talents to multiply once you put them to use. Now look, it's an ancient story right, but it has multiple truths to it. Have you ever seen that people who do well in one area are appointed to lead in many other areas that they are not even experts in? It's crazy, but it's also true. Excellence in one area attracts more opportunities in other areas. Here is how I see it. If you have learnt and mastered the art of growing one talent, you can use the same principles to help others grow in another area.

So why don't you take some time today and write a few notes about the abilities that you have? The natural talents that you have are pointers of the direction you should take with your purpose. Use those pointers to see where you can meet a human need and start applying them.

SHAPE – Embrace Your Personality

According to the American Psychological Association, personality is defined as the individual differences in characteristic patterns of thinking, feeling and behaving. We all have different patterns of thinking, feeling and behaving as part of our makeup. We must understand our personalities as well as those of others if we are to be independent and inter-dependent parts of society. Those who have spent time studying people's behaviours, thoughts and feeling patterns have managed to come up with basic descriptions of personalities that are found in us.

Some people like talking more than others. Some are more inclined to think and come up with innovative and philosophical ideas than others. Some are more action-oriented and therefore feel more motivated and do their best when they are busy at work. We are all wired differently and have ways of operating that suit us best at all times.

It is a big mistake to place an extrovert in a place where they must work alone and produce results in solitude. Whereas, that is the ideal working environment for an introvert. Many tools can assist you in discovering how best you operate, and it is up to you to find them and know how you work. You need to be aware of what makes you tick and work at your best so that you don't try to be what you are not.

Understanding your personality also helps you appreciate other people who are different from you. When you know yourself, you become authentic and confident in who you are. At the same time, you begin to give others the freedom to be who they are and not try to change them to be like you. That gives you the room to lead yourself as well as to lead others.

I have been exposed to several personality test systems, but the one that I consider the best is the Insights Discovery system. Through a questionnaire, the system uses your responses to come up with your personality description and then explains how you think, feel and behave in different circumstances. I was stunned by the results because it was a true description of my personality.

The great thing about the system is that it also tells you what to watch out for and what to capitalise on for best personal and team results. It also helps you understand other different types of personalities and how they behave. I know that I am a helping inspirer, and my biggest personality traits are expressed in my extroversion and feeling. I work well where there are teams and where there is freedom and fun.

Any work that confines me to work alone and where I have to be technical and analytical is a challenge. This helps me to know my blind spots as well as my strengths. It also assists me in choosing team members whenever I have to lead.

I will not go into so much depth on this matter, but I challenge you to discover more about your personality and know what makes you think, feel and behave in a certain way.

Are you an extrovert, introvert, thinker or feeler? What term best describes your dominating behaviours – director, reformer, motivator, inspirer, helper, supporter, coordinator or observer? Are you a sunshine yellow, fiery red, cool blue or earth green? Whichever personality you have, it is great and can work for you, only if you understand it. That self-discovery is one of the best gifts you can ever give to yourself.

SHAPE – Make Use Of Your Past Experiences

A colleague in the Professional Speakers Association of South Africa narrated how she started on her journey as a speaker and councillor for rape victims. She speaks at many platforms around the world to provide guidance and comfort to those who have gone through the terrible experience of rape.

She has written articles and books that help share the story of how such people can be comforted, and she makes a living out of doing just that. However, she was not always a speaker. Speaking was the last thing she thought she would do as a profession, and she never thought she could do so effectively anyway. Rape would be the last subject that she would have chosen if she had selected speaking as a profession.

As she explained how her journey started, there was deep silence in the room. She had been a victim of rape in her late twenties. Two young men who were supposed to help her to get home had changed the usual driving route, went straight into the middle of nowhere, gang-raped her and had left her for dead.

She spoke about how she had to crawl out of the bushes where they had left her and get to the nearest road so that she could find help.

Had it not been for a car that passed by, she would have bled to death after the violation that she went through. The physical and emotional trauma that she went through is not something that she could express adequately in words, but as we listened to her story, we could tell that this was a horrible experience.

Out of that terrible experience, she received support from her family, friends and community until she was strong enough to continue with her life. We know of many stories of people who went through such experiences and ended up deciding to take their lives. Some have gone through this and have not recovered from depression. However, this lady has not only overcome those obstacles. She decided to take it a step further and started speaking about this gross injustice so that she can help reduce the crime. More importantly, she is using her experience to comfort and help other people who have gone through the same.

She says, "If I could survive this, so can you."

She has become a strong voice for many who are voiceless and many who have not even gathered the courage to speak about the abuses that they went through.

Our experiences are the raw materials we can use to process a better future. Every little experience, good or bad, is a part of who we have become and can be used to create more value for us. It is difficult to accept that, but it is true. Nothing that happens to us is wasted experience.

Out of those struggles can come a beautiful story of human resilience and the power of human agency. Imagine a Nelson Mandela without apartheid? Not that apartheid as a system was good, but it equally produced a consciousness of our humanity, resilience and our ability to love and forgive one another. Through that struggle, South Africa birthed the "rainbow nation".

We do not choose everything that happens to us, but we can choose how we react when things happen in our lives. Sometimes, when things happen, we are not even conscious of the wrong that other people are doing. Take child abuse, for example.

There is enough evidence that shows that what happens to a child from the time of infancy up to ten years of age has a huge effect on how they turn out in terms of behaviour. You may have gone through terrible experiences as a kid that you have only come to realise now, but now that you are an adult, you have a choice to make on how that experience is going to affect your future.

What are some of the bad experiences that you have gone through in your life? Have you gathered the courage to talk to someone about those experiences? How can you use that experience to make life better for yourself and those around you? Your experiences are a part of who you have become, and you have to decide how well you will use them.

Nelson Mandela could have chosen revenge as an option after experiencing twenty-seven years in prison, instead, he chose the higher ground of forgiveness and nation-building.

The lady that went through the rape could have chosen to remain a victim of abuse and a host for pity parties, but she took life back into her hands and started speaking out against rape and comforting those who have gone through a similar experience.

What is it that you have in your hands? That is a question that was posed to a man called Moses as he led the children of Israel out of Egypt. They were facing the Red Sea in front of them, and there was a massive army behind them waiting to attack them and take them back into captivity. God asked Moses a concise question. "What do you have in your hand?" In Moses' hand was a stick which God asked Moses to use so that He could display his extraordinary power.

That seemingly useless stick was used to part the waters of the sea and let the children of Israel pass through. The same stick was used to join the waters of the sea when the children of Israel had passed through.

There is something that you have in your hands, and God wants to use it to display his extraordinary power through you. It is your job to find out what that is. You may lack in many things, but you will surely have something that you have been given.

PART 2 – BELIEVE IN YOUR VALUE

"OUR DEEPEST FEAR is not that we are inadequate. Our deepest fear is that we are powerful beyond measure. It is our light, not our darkness that most frightens us. Your playing small does not serve the world. There is nothing enlightened about shrinking so that other people won't feel insecure around you. We are all meant to shine as children do. It's not just in some of us; it is in everyone. And as we let our lights shine, we unconsciously permit other people to do the same. As we are liberated from our fear, our presence automatically liberates others." **Marianne Williamson**

I love this quote so much that I use it in many of my speaking engagements. I also use it when I find myself shying away from greatness or from the things that make me stand out. This quote reminds me that a combination of fears is always fighting my path. One that is usually obvious is the fear of failure.

Fear of failure is so loud that we have no problems identifying it when it comes through. The other subtler and quite sneaky fear is the fear of success. That one is what Marianne Williamson calls the greatest fear. It is deeply seated in the subconscious mind because we have been taught continuously about being normal. Being extraordinary is not the encouraged normal. Being average is what makes us fit in and be like the rest. However, there is a stronger positive consciousness that sits deep inside our conscious mind as well. That which tells us that we are great beyond measure, that we have so much light in us to light up the world if we decide to switch it on. That deeply-seated consciousness also tells us how much power we have. Those who have tapped into that power have found themselves inventing medicines and gadgets that have given us abilities that we never thought we had. Some who have dared to believe in their value have created so much wealth, health, and happiness for themselves and the world, only because they dared to believe in it.

Dr David Schwartz excitingly puts this in his book, '**The Magic of Thinking Big**'. This is how he describes the two opposing thoughts that I have just explained above.

> "Your mind is a 'thought factory'. It's a busy factory, producing countless thoughts in one day. Production in your thought factory is under the charge of two foremen, one of whom we will call Mr Triumph and the other Mr Defeat.

> Mr Triumph is in charge of manufacturing positive thoughts. He specialises in producing reasons why you can, why you're qualified, why you will. The other foreman, Mr Defeat, produces negative, deprecating thoughts. He is your expert in developing reasons why you can't, why you're weak, why you're inadequate. His speciality is the "why-you-will-fail" chain of thoughts.

> Both Mr Triumph and Mr Defeat are intensely obedient. They snap to attention immediately. All you need to signal either foreman is to give the slightest mental beck and call. If the signal is positive, Mr Triumph will step forward and go to work. Likewise, a negative signal brings Mr Defeat forward."

In the first part of the book, we spoke about understanding the value that you have as a person. In this second part, we go beyond understanding and dig deeper into believing in that value. It is one thing to understand, and it is another to believe. Belief is more than just wishful thinking and affirmations that take us nowhere. Belief is the part of us that knows that "we can do it" up to the extent of making us think of ways to make things happen. Belief is not dormant, it is super-active, and it determines not only the actions that we take, but the attitude with which we take those actions. A person who believes in his ability will see failure as a necessary, temporary challenge and thus will keep searching for better ways to get what he wants. He will make use of Mr Triumph and get him to work fully. A person who lacks belief; on the other hand, will activate Mr Defeat to tell him the reason why this challenge is a signal for him to stop the search because this is impossible anyway.

The chapters that follow will explain some of the techniques that you can use to enlarge your belief in your value and suffocate the belief in reasons why you should not make it. Once you master that part, you will be ready to start multiplying what you have in your hands. You will be ready to create extraordinary impact.

Spend Some Time Alone

Our world is getting extremely busy. Everyone is in a rush to go somewhere, watch something, and comment on events. There is so much going on, and sometimes, it takes away our focus and direction. Indeed, we can be busy but less productive, communicating something but not the right message and not effectively enough. This is part of the reason why when we look at our year, we find that we have not achieved much of what **WE** wanted. We seem to be going around in circles. This is because the only time that we had given to ourselves to reflect, dream, pray and set goals is at the beginning of the year. After that, we take everything as it comes.

There is a scripture that says, *"Love your neighbour as you love yourself"*. Part of loving demands that we spend time with the person we love. It also demands that we listen to the other person's need. That way, the beloved person receives our attention and feels valued. Well, the part that we often miss in that scripture is *"as you love yourself"*. Here is a great question. Do we love ourselves enough to spend time alone to listen and value what is coming out of us? When we do not spend this special time alone, we slowly become confused, less confident, less focused and more prone to be tossed by every wind. The opinions of others about us become more critical and louder than our own opinions. A year goes by, and we have done nothing to show that we, indeed, are in love with ourselves.

Here are a few ideas on how you can spend some time on your own and become more productive:

- **Take time to think about what you want to do/achieve the next day/week/month.** For best results, write down a list of all these things so that your mind can take it seriously. This time is crucial because you are listening to what you would want to achieve before anybody else gives you a to-do list. I love what Jim Rohn says about taking time to plan.

'If you don't design your own life's plan, chances are you'll fall into someone else's plan. And guess what they have planned for you? Not much."

- **Take time to reflect on what happened the previous day/week/month.** We must reflect on what is happening in our lives and how it is contributing to who we are becoming. Here are some essential questions that you may want to ask yourself:
  - What did I learn today?
  - What am I grateful for today?
  - How am I feeling about my interaction with different people today?
  - And how can I make it better?

    It is at this time that allows us to see where we went wrong and how we can change. It also shows us what we did right and how we can capitalise on it. The reflection time also helps us become more grateful and to take charge of our reactions to situations.

- **Take some time to pray.** Within your reflection and your goal setting, you will realise that certain things have happened in the past, or that you would want to happen in future, but they are way out of your control. Use this time to talk to God about such things, so that He can take care of them for you. As you take time to submit your worries and concerns to the Higher Power, there is a hard-won peace that comes to you because you are letting go of what you cannot control, and trusting that God will take care of it.

You may be in a place where you do not believe in the existence of God, but this also applies to you. You need to let go of things that are out of your control and trust that they will be taken care of. Worrying about the past and being anxious about the future can be dangerous. It can cause illnesses such as depression and unfavourable behaviours that lead to addictions of every nature. All this *"because we do not carry everything to God in prayer"*.

- **Take time to enrich your mind/soul**. It is essential that we reflect on a divine and encouraging word that takes us into the day. In case you haven't noticed, there is so much negativity going on in the world. The news headlines that are catchy and loud are not usually positive. It's generally about people dying in a terrible accident, markets going down, politicians fighting and wars around the globe. Even on social media, bad news seems to travel faster.

Before your day begins, you need to take some time to read the good news! You need to read or listen to something enlightening and strengthening.

We certainly cannot avoid the bad things that are happening in our world, but we need to be armed with the positive, so we can conquer our personal, family, business, national, and global battles. Take time to study a book of inspiration and arm yourself with the great news, so that you don't run out of weapons to conquer in your world.

There could be more things to do in your "me time", but the ideas above, repeated consistently over time will make us become better entrepreneurs, spouses, parents, leaders, and whatever else we are called to be in life. Here's to you!

Your Opinion Matters!

There is a reason why you exist on this earth. There is a reason why you are part of a team, a local community, nation and, indeed, a part of this world. You are different, and have a unique way of doing things and thinking about issues. Your uniqueness or difference in opinion to others is what feeds into a diverse world, which if united and tolerant, produces magical results for all of us.

Depending on how you grew up, there is a subconscious view that is built-in you that makes you value or not value who you are. Specific practices that were meant to teach us to respect our elders could have subconsciously taught us that our views were less important than people who were older than us. The same could have been indirectly taught to us about people in authority at schools, in the workplaces and our governments. Years later, when we now have a chance to sit in the boardroom and contribute meaningfully to the workplace, or when we are now put in positions of authority, or when we become parents, our childhood belief systems kick in. It could be that we now start doubting our abilities, ideas and views. Society seemed to be telling us that our views didn't matter until we reached a certain age, attained a specific qualification, and have a title to our name. This has the potential to mess up our role as leaders in two different ways.

The first way is that we keep postponing our value and what we have to offer. That book is never written because there is something that still has to be done before we are called authors. The *app.* idea that you wanted to develop is postponed until you programming degree. The lesson that should be taught to the kids is also postponed until you attend several courses on parenting. The daring and adventurous attitude of a leader is weakened because we are waiting for some affirmation, some voice to tell us that we are now qualified and capable to contribute meaningfully to our role.

The second way that this affects us is that we end up looking down upon those who have not attained what we have managed to reach The perception of a person with a degree is better received than that of a general worker without a degree. Although they may have game-changing ideas and capabilities, we fail to receive contributions from the younger generation because that's what has been instilled in us. Ultimately, we miss out on the diverse ideas that could have come out of these young people. The same could be said about receiving opinions from people of a different race, gender, or nationality. We could have some stereotypes that were built over time.

Such views, then, threaten our potential as leaders. Many African nations are suffering from this kind of leadership. In some instances, such practices and beliefs are spread out to families and even in places of worship. Do our spaces allow for dialogue, debate and questioning of ideas to take place? Or does communication take place in one direction and feedback not fully received and accepted? We must start unlearning some of these beliefs and start engaging more productive and true ideas into our lives.

The truth of the matter is that you are essential, and you have value as a human being! Before you attain degree, and even before you reach a particular profession, you already have something of value to offer the world! You already have a unique value that cannot be copied by anyone in the world! Within our personalities lies an inexplicable treasure, well-thought out and properly placed. This has to sink into our belief system because once we realise this value that we have, we would stop trying to hide our lights under tables while the world is looming in the darkness. We would not be afraid of bringing our views and ideas to the table in the board rooms, work teams and our families. We would be fully confident, and that would give us the edge to be more successful, adventurous, to try more and work harder to achieve our dreams. The procrastination that kills our dreams would be thrown out of the window. We need to know that our opinions, our thoughts and ideas matter in this world. They deserve a chance to be tested and heard. It is only when we value ourselves that we can become fully productive staff members, students, entrepreneurs, leaders and amazing active citizens of our nations. When we know that what we are thinking and saying is necessary, we will fight to be heard even in oppressive government systems. When we know that our ideas can change the industry game, we become persistent in trying them in the market. When we take heed to our Creator when He said, *"This is good"* at creation, we walk with our heads held high. When we know that we are *"fearfully and wonderfully made"*, that we were known before we were formed in our mother's bellies, we think and act differently.

The same knowledge will make us respect our differences. It will make us value one another. It will make us build diverse teams that are way more productive. It will create a more tolerant and peaceful world for us. In many ways, it will enable us to take different opinions, ideas and to use the differences to build more useful products and services in our workplaces. When we start believing the truth that we were ALL created in God's image and therefore are all "God carriers, stand-ins and viceroys", as the Archbishop Desmond Tutu would call it; when we truly value and believe that TRUTH, we would be tolerant, loving, respectful, and way more productive citizens.

This is to say that **YOU** are important and **YOUR** opinion matters in this world! *Zvikoshese*. *Wakakosha*. (You are important, so treat yourself as such.)

The Power Of Meditation

There is power in our thoughts, particularly the thoughts that are continually residing in our minds. A lot of research has been done in this area — to show that we become what we always think about. Meditation – a process of concentrated and continuous thought, is one way in which we can take advantage of thought to create the environment we desire for success.

Here are some powerful ancient quotes about "thinking/meditating" and my brief modern-day interpretation of each of them. Enjoy it!

- *"As a man thinketh, so is he."* - **King Solomon.** We are what we continuously, passionately, and repeatedly think about.
- **"Life's battles don't always go to the stronger or faster man, but sooner or later, the man who wins is the one who thinks he can." - Walter D Wintle.** The man who thinks he can will not stop trying until he does. The one who thinks he can't stop trying once a few setbacks come in his way. Which mindset do you have in your area of influence? Do you genuinely believe that you were meant to do this? It's worth taking time to convince your mind and heart that you are the one the world is waiting for! Let your meditation time be filled and consumed with this thought. Anything contrary to this will cause you to fail.
- **"All achievements, whether in the business, intellectual, or spiritual world, are the result of definitely directed thought. They are governed by the same law and are of the same method. The only difference lies in the object of attainment." - By James Allen.** Let's set this

straight. This is a universal law! Our thought world will rule our real world, anywhere and everywhere! This is what we do when we discover a universal law. We study and master it so that it works for us. Ignoring the law of gravity will not make us escape it! Did we get it right? Awesome!

- **"If you think you are beaten, you are, if you think you dare not, you don't. If you'd like to win, but you think you can't, it is almost certain; you won't." - Water D Wintle.** By inference, if you think you have won, you have. If you think you need to give yourself a chance, you will. If you come out thinking like a winner each day, it is almost certain that you will win! What are you doing to convince yourself each day that you are a winner in your area?

- **"You cannot keep birds from flying over your head, but you can keep them from building a nest in your hair." - Martin Luther.** Negative thoughts will always come into your mind. They often visit us once in a while, but to stay in continuous self-pity and pessimism is our choice. In the same way, positive thoughts about what we can do will constantly visit in equal proportion. Wise is the man who constantly and consciously invites positive thoughts and allows them to create a nest of positive energy, great business plans, joy, peace, health, wealth, and happiness.

Let's keep winning the first battle every day. The other battles will be more comfortable.

Number Your Victories – Key To Slaying Giants In Your Life

The young boy looked at the big man who was busy insulting his whole clan. He looked at his brothers and the rest of the team and could see that they were as scared as hell! This huge man was inviting them to choose just one of them to represent the boy's team in a fight. That fight would determine who had to call the shots. Suddenly, the young boy remembered. This was not the first big thing that he had confronted in his life. While he was on his own, he had confronted monsters and killed them with his bare hands. He had confronted these giant animals while no one was watching, but that victory counted for something in his memory. The young boy, David, went on to tell the king about his exploits, he had the opportunity of his life, and killed the giant, Goliath, who had given the Israelites a hard time for a long time. Have you heard of this story before?

One of the lessons that I pick up from this old story is this: **YOU NEED TO COUNT AND KNOW YOUR PAST VICTORIES!** There are challenges that you have faced in your life, things that could have killed you, but you are still here, standing as a winner. You have faced personal and corporate battles for you to be here, and yes, you might have lost in many battles, but you also won some. Do you know the victories that you have experienced? You see, your confidence is a significant factor in your development journey. It is worth building and guarding as you present yourself in the marketplace. It is not enough to have a skill, qualification or high-quality product. For your strengths to start rewarding you, you need to know them.

One of the ways to build your organisational, community or individual confidence is to take note of your victories and celebrate them. No one will ever celebrate your achievements in the same way that you can!

We need to realise that positive energy is a resource that is useful to fuel our present and future actions. At the same time, positive energy is a scarce resource that needs to be extracted, processed, and directed correctly for it to achieve results for us. One of the best ways to extract this positive energy is through gratitude! We need to learn to take note of where we have done well and celebrate those victories! As you take your time alone today, here are a few questions that you can ask yourself so that you may number your victories. Take your time, and write these notes down.

- List five things that you (or your company) have accomplished that you're proud of.
- What challenges did you (or your company) have to overcome for you to accomplish these things?

As you write these notes down, your subconscious mind is being reminded, once again, that you are a champion, so that on the day that you face your Goliath, you don't run away. You talk about your past victories, and you confront your giant, knowing fully well that you will succeed.

Here is one of my answers to these questions.

- In 2009, I overcame my fear of public speaking and challenged myself to get into the JCI Public speaking competition. I ended up as the World's Public Speaking finalist and a regional champion that year. I used that story to motivate me to overcome my fear of publishing articles on LinkedIn in 2018! At this point, I had written my fourth article, and I'm still going.

What are some of your past victories? Go ahead and write these down, because that's how we overcome negativity and take one more step forward!

Embrace Who You Are – Dedicated To The Black African Child

I want to dedicate this particular part of my writing to my fellow black African brothers and sisters, and in doing so, I hope that the message reaches out to the rest of the world as our circumstances might be similar. This is my assessment of where we are. As Africans, we are in a place where our generation has taken everything that is western/foreign as tremendous and anything that is African as undesirable. We have a history where other nations took advantage of us and made us doubt who we are as people. Our measure of intelligence is how well people can speak in English, French, or Portuguese. Mastery of our native languages does not carry much weight. The better we speak these foreign languages, the better we perceive ourselves to be. We dismiss our people based on this extremely unfair measure, which we have placed on ourselves subconsciously. We can comfortably accommodate the Japanese, Chinese, or German people who do not understand English very well.

"It is not their mother tongue," we say, but we do not give ourselves the same freedom as black brothers and sisters. Something happened to our self-esteem over the past hundreds of years that made us want to aspire to be who we are not. In our sight, our hair is not good enough and the lighter our skin, the better we look; as it is closer to white. If we woke up and had been accidentally changed to white people, many of us would be happy, as we have learnt to love everything outside ourselves. This description might be too general and certainly not accurate, but it describes where we are as a people in terms of our self-esteem.

To prove my point and back it up with some evidence, let me give an example of a business networking meeting where I happened to be the only black person in the room. The topic of discussion in that room was '**Doing business in Africa**'. Most people in the room talked about their experiences of doing business in the African region. There is one comment that was made that I will never forget. The speaker talked about how the black Africans have so much respect for the white people, and how they gave them so much credit, to the speaker's surprise. He admitted that sometimes this credit is given undeservedly. He encouraged his fellow brothers and sisters and told them how much value the white skin has when doing business in Africa. As I listened to this, my heart bled. The man was correct. The battle of the mind hasn't been won yet.

A few weeks later, I went to Japan and experienced life there for about two weeks. Here is a nation that was never colonised. We were introduced to Japanese history and culture by the Japanese people; they proudly taught us their language, and we ate their traditional food. Most of them could not speak English, but that was okay. Their children were taught using their native language in their special writing. They have modernised their culture and developed the unique technologies that have empowered them economically, but have not lost their native practices. I sensed in them a great sense of pride in who they are, in their history and culture. Some of the food that I ate there reminded me of the traditional African dishes that I have at home. They sell them in their high-end restaurants and make money.

My experience of the natural hot springs in Kumamoto was unique to Japan. My host father in Japan took me to a communal spring, and I enjoyed the time there. There were specific practices there that I could tie down to them as people, and yet this was a business place as well. I remembered how the average middle-class black

African quickly disassociates himself from everything native in search of something different as it makes him feel better that he no longer eats traditional food from his home. He has associated it with poverty and strife. He has embraced the "*dark continent*" term subconsciously, and he wishes circumstances could be different.

We need to escape this dangerous trapping of the mind and begin to see ourselves as normal and adequate human beings. We need to start seeing our fellow brothers and sisters in that light as well. African history is also distorted.

Unless we, as a corporate body of the African black community begin to understand and believe in ourselves, we cannot break new ground and go beyond our self-belief, self-confidence and self-esteem. We need to be conscious of who God made us to be. There are specific things about us that make us different and positively so.

Part of my struggle in writing and publishing this book had to do with my feeling of inadequacy. I told myself that I had to read as many articles from elsewhere so that I could validate my views. Although this is my book, with my views and opinions, I struggled to believe that my views alone would pass the test and make it into a book. That means I took longer to write because I lacked sufficient self-belief. I had to step out of it and remind myself that my views matter. That I too, am made in the image of God, I am fearfully and wonderfully made, and there is something unique and special that was deposited in me. There are some things that you can only find in me, and I have to believe in those things and come out and give them to the rest of the world.

Now, I know that there are many others out there, from different races, creeds, colours and backgrounds who may be going through the same things. Let me reaffirm you. The whole world is waiting for your manifestation. You are a unique gift to the world. Come out of your shell and give the world what you have. Step out of your comfort zone and try new things.

Here are some points about how we embrace who we are.

- **Find stories about your history that empower you.** Write about these stories and talk about them. There is no race without a dark past, just as there is no one who can claim that they haven't failed. However, it is what we choose to pick and emphasise about our history that will make or break us.
  What is it about King Shaka, Mbuya Nehanda, Lobengula, Mandela, Kwame Nkurumah, Samora Machel, that stands out for you? There is a process called "**Appreciative Inquiry (AI)**" that we need to use when we examine our past. We ask questions about what makes the black African race tick. What makes us so warm, loving, human focused, musical, spiritual, and so on. This not only helps us to be happy with who we are but also enables us to imagine what we could be. What is it about your family that makes you positively unique? Then value that, take pictures of it and tell the stories to yourself and your children.
- **Become a critical thinker.** Not everything that you hear is true. Not everything that's written in a book or newspaper is also true. You have to do the digging yourself. Who said this, and what were their motives and perspective? Which lenses did they use to come up with such a point of view? It is ridiculous to believe that our competitors will always see the best in us in the

survival battles of business, sport, politics, and science. Even when the religious views come up, question them. God did not give you the mind so that you would take in whatever is thrown at you and run with it. Use it to analyse and question systems that have been put in place. When you become objective, you cease to be naive, and you won't be afraid to implement change.

- **Embrace diversity.** Part of embracing diversity is embracing the authentic YOU. Let's give ourselves the freedom to be different too, and allow others to value that difference and embrace it. No one will ever love what we do not feel proud of.
- **Embrace your own culture and identity.** What is it that is uniquely strong about us as black African people? Let's share those points.

Destroy Limiting Beliefs About God

It is great to know that you have the spirit of a winner within you. What is more significant is to know the source of that greatness. When you know that source, you become unlimited in your thinking and unstoppable in what you do. That source is the Almighty God who created you. You did not just appear from nowhere. You are fearfully and wonderfully made. You were known way before you were formed in your mother's womb. Not only where you known, but you had a mission on earth, to solve some of the most pressing challenges of our time as you fulfil God's purpose.

As I say this, I know that there are mental blocks that start appearing in many people's lives. This is not the first time you hear this, but somehow it is difficult to believe this. What makes it hard to believe is all that we have heard about God that has made us conclude that either He is not there, or if He is there, He does not care about us and only cares about how we should behave on earth. Many people have this image of a person who holds a stick right behind you, waiting to spank you whenever you do something wrong and to reward you whenever you do something right. That is the image they have of God. Another image that has been created indirectly through religious practices is of a God whose love and favour can be bought. These are all lies that are meant to limit us from knowing our Dad and best friend.

I have therefore decided to talk about these limiting beliefs so that we can replace them with the truth about God that will leave us functioning as He does. So here we go.

1. **God is not looking for your sins.** Your past, present and future mistakes do not surprise God at all. He is not out to get you for the things that you have done wrong. He knows your

abilities and also knows your limitations. King David said this about him in Psalms 103 verse 8-14.

> 8 The LORD is compassionate and gracious,
> slow to anger, abounding in love.
> 9 He will not always accuse,
> nor will he harbour his anger forever;
> Ten he does not treat us as our sins deserve
> or repay us according to our iniquities.
> 11 For as high as the heavens are above the earth,
> so great is his love for those who fear him;
> 12 as far as the east is from the west,
> so far has he removed our transgressions from us.
>
> 13 As a father has compassion on his children,
> so the LORD has compassion on those who fear him;
> 14 for he knows how we are formed,
> he remembers that we are dust.

David was a shepherd boy who rose to become one of the most influential kings of his generation. His value in Israel went up from being the lowest paid worker and the least valued in his family to become the wealthiest and most powerful man in his land. He produced so much value in the songs that he wrote, in his courage as a soldier and an army commander, and in his great wisdom that came from the fear of the Lord. God even called him "a person after my own heart". God decided to fulfil His plans of bringing everlasting salvation to the world through the descendants of King David. His beliefs about God are, therefore, worth looking at. He says that God's love is unlimited, and it goes as high as the heavens are above the earth. That's to say we cannot comprehend the love that He has for you and I.

Our minds cannot conceive the greatness of His love towards us. Not only is His love unlimited, but it supersedes our weaknesses because He remembers that we are dust. King David lived in the dispensation of the law, and so one would think that he would have had an image of a God who was waiting to punish wrong. However, he saw past the law and understood the heart of the intentions of God towards humankind. That built a powerful belief system that made him add value to Israel and become a great man. When you read the book of Psalms, you begin to see how healthy his self-talk had become because of the image that he had of himself and his God. I discovered this verse when I was a teenager, just reading through the Psalms of David. As I read through this part, I just had to stop and reread it. Psalms 18:29 says:

"**For** **by You, I can crush a troop, And by my God, I can leap over a wall."**

No wonder why David had the courage and confidence to face Goliath when all of Israel was afraid of even facing the giant. His faith (belief in God) was so strong and personal to him. God was not a distant father waiting to shout orders to the young David. He was David's protector, provider and his loving Father. He drew all his strength from the knowledge that he had a father who could do everything. Just as any child believes that his father can beat anyone and can protect him, that is the faith you and I ought to have in Him. That way, we can kill our giants of poverty, disease, hunger, violence and all the pressing challenges of our lifetime.

The good news is that God sent His Son, Jesus Christ, to die for our sins (past, present and future) so that you and I can live without any condemnation but can have eternal life in abundance. I therefore encourage you to develop a healthy image of your source and your Creator and to shut out all the noise that comes from people who have lost faith in a God who loves us unconditionally.

David understood God's love from an early age to such an extent that his relationship with God became more real to him than the one he had with his earthly father. He understood that his earthly father's love was limited but his heavenly father's love, where he truly came from, was unlimited. When his earthly father, Jesse, was asked to bring his sons before the prophet Samuel so that a king would be chosen among them, David was left out. The father did not think that David had that much value in him to become a king or a ruler, and so it was alright to have the rest of the brothers on the list. That shows us Jesse's limited love. That does not mean Jesse did not love his son, it just shows that he was human, and so he was limited in his love.

In the same way, we should not compare how people close to us love us to God's love. God sees you when no one can even see you on the list. He remembers you all the time. He even knows the number of hairs on your head.

"Indeed, the very hairs of your head are all numbered. Don't be afraid; you are worth more than many sparrows." Luke 12:7.

Where people may forget your name and your significance, He knows that you are of so much value to Him and the world. When you understand this, and it goes right down into your subconscious mind, you will not only attain freedom and rest, but a world of endless possibilities will begin to open. The limiting beliefs will start leaving you. The lion in you will begin to roar.

2. God is not silent. He speaks

We are wired in such a way that we can hear God speak to us all the time, but religion has made it look like we have to work hard for us to talk to our Daddy. To add to that, some who profit from the business of talking about God have made it look complicated and exclusive to men and women who spend time in the mountains starving themselves for God to speak to them. The truth is that God is our Father, and He loves us too much to shut His mouth when we need to hear His voice. When you begin to see Him using the lenses of love, your life will never be the same.

I like what the apostle James said in James 1:16-17.

"Do not be deceived, my beloved brothers. Every good and perfect gift is from above, coming down from the Father of the heavenly lights, with whom there is no change or shifting shadow."

If every good and perfect gift is from God, then we are receiving gifts from Him every single day. If He freely gives the gifts such as fresh air and the ability to breathe, why would He withhold talking to us? I want to share with you the ways that God speaks to us and how simple it should be to hear Him communicate His love for us every single day. When we get to know this amazing truth, we will not wait unnecessarily in confusion, but will get the necessary guidance that helps us decide in our lives.

Firstly, God speaks to us through our mind. Using the statement that apostle James made, we can conclude that every good thought comes from God. The apostle Paul encouraged the Philippians to cultivate this kind of thinking.

"Finally, brothers and sisters, whatever is **true**, whatever is **noble**, whatever is **right**, whatever is **pure,** whatever is **lovely,** whatever is **admirable** — if anything **is excellent or praiseworthy** — think about such things and the God of peace will be with you." Philippians 4:8.

An idea that comes to your head about how you can help someone to get better convenience is a God-inspired thought. He also inspires a curiosity that you have about how a community problem of transportation can be solved. It is a noble and right idea. When you begin to think like this, you realise that He has been inspiring great thoughts in your life for as long as you can remember anything in your life. I like what Dr Myles Munroe said about talking to God in one of his sermons called '**The power of Discipline**'. In that sermon, he said that:

"The voice of God is so simple. We ignore it because it's not sophisticated enough. When the man of God says, 'God spoke to me'" all they are saying is that '*I had an idea, that wouldn't go away*'. When you think about it this way, you will realise that

your very makeup or design as a human being is meant to be talking to God daily. We do not realise that He is giving us this inspiration every single day.

God also speaks to us through the scriptures and other people. There is so much to be said about that, but I just wanted to demystify the way God speaks to us and show that He is always willing to communicate with us as any loving father would long to be in touch with his children.

Destroy Self-Limiting Beliefs

It is essential to realise that no matter how talented or educated we are, if we do not believe deep in our hearts that we can take ourselves to the next level, the talent and education will go to waste. No matter how much passion we have to drive a specific cause, if we do not believe that we are the people who can change the situation, we will not get up to it. We can also have tonnes of experience in our field of expertise, but without the belief that we can use that in our businesses, we will forever remain stuck in employment.

What is a belief? The oxford dictionary defines belief as "something one accepts as true or real; a firmly held opinion." As can be seen in the example that we gave about the elephant and the lion, our belief determines what we do and how far we go.

So since belief is fundamental, let us discover how beliefs come to *being*:

1. **Through the words that are spoken to us**. A child who grew up being told that he is a "fool" will likely believe this to be true. This is why we must speak the right words to our children, because they will believe what we tell them, and that will determine how far they go in life. It is also important to note what we say about our communities, or race and our continent. The mental constructs we build determine what we can try. For a long time, Africa has been given different names by people but it is important for us to say what we want to see.

2. **Through the experiences that we go through:** Sometimes, it is not what people say that limits our belief in ourselves. Sometimes it is through a single experience or repeated experiences of failure or limitation that beliefs are formed. Experiencing hardships at an early age in life is likely to create a

reality in mind. The same goes for experiencing abundance in life. It is true that most successful entrepreneurs grow up in an entrepreneurial family and are often sent to work within family businesses as they grow. In the same way, people that grow up in families and communities where crime is rampant are most likely to end up in crime as well.

3. **Through association or observation**. There is always a place for role models in life. Some of them are chosen, but some are given to us by default. We do not choose who our parents are or the country in which we are born. However, whoever is responsible for bringing us into this world and taking care of us has a huge responsibility in shaping what we believe about our life and our circumstances. I am sure we have heard many award winners say every time: "I would like to thank my mom and dad for believing in me and supporting my vision."

As you can see, a major part of our belief system is established in our formative years. We do not have a choice over how it is built. It is therefore essential for us to take some time to examine our belief system, to continue with empowering beliefs about who we are and destroy beliefs that make us sabotage our efforts towards success. How do we identify self-limiting beliefs? These also come with symptoms that can be conspicuous.

1. Stagnancy – When there is no growth taking place in some areas of our lives.
2. Fear – When we are constantly afraid of certain situations or possibilities.
3. Anxiety – A state of constant worry about a situation.
4. Stress and Depression – This often arises because of perceived reality and fear of what is going to happen.

Although our beliefs are mostly developed in our formative years, once we start being independent, we need to take charge of how our beliefs are formed. We can no longer blame anyone for who we become. Just as it took some time to get these beliefs built into our subconscious mind, it also takes some time to build more empowering beliefs. The Apostle Paul encouraged the Romans to not conform to the pattern of this world, but to be transformed by the renewal of their minds. Romans 12:2. We must take steps to renew our thinking and here is how we can use his advice.

1. We need to change what we **hear** about ourselves. As we saw earlier, the words spoken to and about us in our formative years have a way of forming our self-belief — now knowing that we need to change what we hear about ourselves. The best place to start is to change what we say about ourselves. You are the most influential person in your life — what you say about who you are carries more weight than what anyone else can say about you. Your self-talk is, therefore, a great place to start.

   Listening to your inner critic has a place in life. However, when the inner critic becomes the dominant voice in your life, you begin to sabotage yourself. So how do you change what you say to yourself? I listen to God's word. That is the source of my renewal. I listen to what God says about me through His word, and I repeat that to myself. God is the only person who sees beyond our failures and calls the things in us that have not yet been manifested. He knows who we are and how much potential we have inside of us. It is not a mistake that after He created man, He said, "this is good". It is also by no mistake that He chose to create us in His likeness, meaning we don't just look like Him, but we function like Him.

So, my subconscious mind has to listen to an empowering sermon every day. Out of all the disciples of Jesus, John figured this out quite early. He told himself that he was the "disciple whom Jesus loved". He personalised Jesus' love for him, and that made him a firm believer. What do you tell yourself every morning? What do you tell your kids each day? Take a moment to write about yourself today and make sure that it is all in the present, and it is positive. Speak words that show the desired person — repeating that every day will transform how you think about yourself.

2. We need to interpret our experiences correctly. Just because you have failed does not mean you are now a failure. Just because you made a mistake and stole, that does not make you a thief. **You are not your past mistakes.** Your past mistakes or failures should not determine the future that you have ahead of you. The past is a portion of your life, not the rest of your future. You need to let go of goals that you didn't achieve. Don't take that into the next year. Your past is as alive as the life you give it. The past should only be used for educational references, but you should not live in that.

Don't let it become a weight that pulls you down. There is so much that lies within you that you have not yet tapped into. You have only seen the signs of it and the SHAPE process will help you see the seeds of it. When you see these seeds, you need to put them in the right ground so that they can germinate and start growing forests of wealth, health, and happiness for you. Start talking about those seeds and the future that they will bring. Soon enough, the future's pulling force will overcome the weight of the past, and you will be on your way to building a healthy self-image.

3. You need to surround yourself with people whose life will empower and inspire you. As we learnt about role models that we used to see every day, we need to start consciously choosing the people with whom we hang out. You may not choose your family, but you can select your friends. In adult life, most of our influence ceases to come from our families, but now comes from the people that we put in our inner circle. Their belief system and their choices affect our own decisions, too. You, therefore, need to rid of toxic people in your life who make you feel unwanted, inferior and small. Get out of abusive relationships. Remember that abuse does not start in the physical; it begins with words. The dangerous part about verbal abuse is that you cannot block it when it's coming your way. Therefore, you need to get out of situations where others continuously diminish your value or worth. Surround yourself with people that build you up.

Some workplaces are toxic too, if you end up feeling worthless and unappreciated. Protect your soul and get out as soon as you get the next best opportunity. The surprising thing about the association is that it is compelling and yet subtle. You may not see yourself going in the wrong direction, but you slowly move towards that wrong direction until you are now at the wrong destination.

PART 3 – EQUIP YOURSELF

ONCE YOU HAVE understood and believed in your value, you have given yourself a gift that many people lack. Just by knowing and believing, you can start moving mountains. However, the change in your life will be slow unless you multiply that value with different factors. These are the factors that we are going to talk about in this third section of the book.

One illustration that explains how we can multiply our value is told by Dr Mensa Otabil in his book called '**The Value of the Dot**'. He uses the story told by Jesus in the Bible, where a master was about to leave on a journey, and so he entrusted some talents to three of his servants. The first was given one talent, the second was given two talents, and the last was given five talents. They were supposed to take good care of these talents or goods until the master's return.

When the master returned, he found that there were two who had invested the talents well and had doubled the number, and there was one who had done nothing about it. As a result, what he had was given to one who could deliver value. Now, let us use this story to illustrate the importance of multiplication.

1.000000000
2.000000000
5.000000000

The numbers above represent the talents that these three were given. As you can see, after each value, I have placed a dot and nine zeros after that. Now say that this represents the different value of gifts and talents that we received in life. We start at different levels. However, we can use specific tools to move the value we have been given, from 1 to 10 or 100 or 1000 by changing the placing of the dot. Have a look at the second set of numbers.

1000000.000
2000.000000
50.00000000

The values have changed, although the numbers used are the same. The first number had the least value in the first example but now has the highest value, simply because of the movement of the dot. The movement of the dot symbolises the multiplication of what is given to us. The person who multiplies their value with the right tools can end up leading the people who had more than he had at the beginning. In the same way, there are tools that we can use to multiply the value that we have and create more value regardless of where we come from.

In this third to the fifth part of the book, I explain the factors that can multiply the value that we have. These can take us from a place of mediocrity to a place of significance. For now, here are the four Es of attaining Personal Excellence.

The Four Es Of Personal Excellence

EDUCATION – THE FIRST KEY TO UNLOCKING THE TREASURE IN YOU

A few years ago, I sent out a quote that read: "*Stop hunting for jobs. Start hunting for the treasure in you and nurture it. Soon enough, head hunters will find you.*" I then highlighted four keys that are important for that treasure hunt. These are **Education, Experience, Exposure, and Execution.** These four keys are loaded if fully utilised. We will see it as we unpack them in the next few pages.

The first one is Education. For this book, we will define this as the process of acquiring knowledge or skills. There are three categories of education that I would like to unpack. These are **Formal** education, **Self-education,** and **Values Based** education.

- **FORMAL EDUCATION.** This is the most common way to educate oneself, which is through going to school and obtaining a qualification. It is pre-determined learning in formal learning institutions. It comes with a curriculum that hardly changes and is often technical and specialised.

  This is education at its foundational and lowest level. It is structured and found in a system created over many years, designed to give you knowledge and skills in the form of a qualification that you can use **to get a** job. When we see the title CA (SA), we know what you have gone through in terms of education, experience, and exposure of a Chartered Accountant. When we see a PHD in front of your name, we know that you are a great researcher and analyst, and that's why they call you doctor. The list is endless, but the principle is the same.

We may deny it all we want, but the truth is that formal education works in our world system and you ignore it at your peril. In the job market, you may be unknown, but your papers will introduce you better. They will tell your prospective employer or prospective client about the process that you have gone through, where you went through it and how well you ticked the boxes that prepared you to be a professional in that field.

There is a trend of thought that seems to disqualify the importance of formal qualification. As much as it is desirable, this education system is in place, and it will take a long time to rid of it, so one might as well get used to it. There might be a few entrepreneurs who make it as school dropouts, but they still make use of it through other people in their organisations. Most of them (like Andrew Carnegie) continue to fund the development of formal education as a way to give back to society. Formal education is one of the things that can take you from a place of obscurity to a place of prominence.

Here is what's critical about getting ahead in this market of formally educated people.

- The **quality of your grades** - In the job market and even at educational institutions, your grades say a lot about you and determine whether you get a slot or not. In South Africa, if your Matric is not of a certain level, chances of getting to university are slim. Other top universities in many countries and universities use GMAT to rate your ability to communicate and work out complex problems. It works that way in many other countries as well. One, therefore, has to do the best to secure the best place, all things being equal.
- **The institution** you obtain your qualification. When the name Oxford, Harvard or Stanford comes up, it raises interest in the job market. The same applies to different institutions in different countries. From a young age, parents have to choose carefully in

which institutions they put their kids, because like it or not, it will count in the job market. Certain schools are known for producing high-class academics; some for their ability to place their graduates in high-earning jobs or networks. As an adult, one also has to choose with this in mind when looking to thrive or at the very least, get doors to open in the job market. If this is your path of choice, make sure you choose the best possible institution and work as hard to attain fantastic grades.

- **Accreditation and Examining Boards** – This is also important when choosing the course or institution you will take. It will determine how well your qualification is received in the marketplace. How well-received are the course and the board that regulates it? It has a lot to do with credibility.
- **The choice of programs that you take.** The subjects that you decide to specialise in have a huge effect on what you will know, what future doors will be open for you, and how much you will enjoy the process of formal education. It is important to choose subjects that are in your area of strength and passion, and also to take note of subjects that will not restrict future opportunities.

Formal education might be useful, but it also has its limitations. Not everybody is academically inclined, and not everybody wants a job. Also, jobs have an income cap on them. However, there is no doubt that formal education gives some competitive advantage in opening opportunities. Formal education may not make you a fortune, but it will make you a living. It is by far the most widely used tool to pull people out of extreme poverty. Don't you worry, there is more! We will go on to talk about another exciting form of education in the next section.

- **SELF-EDUCATION.** In the preceding topic, I talked about formal education and its role in increasing your value in the marketplace. Here is another form of education that has the potential to increase the value of people and organisations around you dramatically.

Self-education is a learning process driven by the learner according to what he or she determines as they need at that time. It is directed towards attaining specific knowledge and with it comes certain skills and competencies that open great doors. Often, general and broad in its scope, it comes through reading books, attending conferences, researching on the internet, networking, mentorship/sponsorship relationships etc. Here is an interesting quote from Jim Rohn on the two forms of education that I have mentioned.

"Formal education will make you a living; self-education will make you a fortune."

There are several options on the menu. We often hear stories about multi-billionaires who are high school/university drop-outs. Mostly, they would have used this form of education to move ahead. This is a self-teaching method that makes them know what's relevant to their business and their market at the time. Most entrepreneurs do not learn in formal institutions, but use this method.

Most people depend on formal education to move ahead, especially in the job market, but those that thrive to go a step further take on self-education as a tool to produce more. There is something that happens when you meet people at conferences; something that tells you that you can do the same, and it inspires you to try it out. The same goes for books.

Here is what you need to do for you to achieve personal excellence in this area. Read as much as you can. Devour the books in your area of passion/profession and know more than the average person. That knowledge will help you move ahead. Set goals for attending conferences in the year, write down how many books you will read and develop that culture. Create good mentorship networks, and then you are on your way to perfecting this art.

I have worked with, observed, and interviewed many successful entrepreneurs and leaders, and I can safely say that all of them had a high level of curiosity that pushed them to find information in their areas of speciality. Those who were not great at reading books were smart enough to employ or consult with those who did. They were part of professional networks that taught them how to lead and conduct business. I can also say the same about growing organisations that I have worked with. There is a deep culture of learning that allows them to discover what they need to do to reach ahead.

Here are **a few ideas to improve self-education** and allow the process to increase your value.

- First, you need to choose an area of focus. What is it that you want to develop? I cannot emphasise how important this is. If you do not focus, this process will not benefit you that much.
- Find out if there are any professional organisations that you can join that help you in that area.
- Join online networks of those organisations. Most have newsletters and chat groups that inform you about your chosen field.
- Find out who the best players in the industry are and where they hang out. That's your new benchmark. If they can mentor you, take it up.
- Read. Whatever area you want to focus on, there are several books on that subject. Consume them. Before you know it, you will know enough to get you going. There are also audiobooks available; seminar recordings as well. Some are available for free online.

Go wild in your search for knowledge, and you will be amazed at who you will become.
- Try out the things you are learning. You learn more as you apply something that you are learning.

Formal education will open doors of opportunities; self-education will help you thrive in those areas. Although you may not have a certificate to show that you know, people around you will notice that you know more through the results you achieve. With self-education, you learn at your own pace, you are in control of the whole process, and there are no limits to what you can know. There are no limits to what you can achieve as well.

Values-Based Education

Values-based education is learning inspired by principles, standards, beliefs or morals. It affects the daily choices we make and the way we relate with ourselves and others. It often gets very little attention, and yet has so much control and power in the way we work. As people who want to create positive change in our societies, we should be aware of the values that have shaped us and then choose the values that will take us forward. In this section, we will discuss the source of values, the impact they have on us, and what we can do to choose great values that can take us forward.

There are three main places where values emanate. The first source of values is **family**. When we were born, we became attached to our parents, guardians, siblings and cousins. These are the people who were responsible for shaping how we behaved and thought.

During those early formative years, certain habits or beliefs were picked up. The family is foundational in the building of who we become. Growing up in a pastor's house in the rural areas, one of the things that I remember well is that we used to welcome many people to come and stay with us or visit our home. No one would leave our house without something to eat. No one was preferred over the other. The older people were respected. When I reflect on that, I think it gave me a sense of how vital/sacred all human beings are. It also gave me a sense of how important it is to be a hospitable and welcoming family. It is also the same family that introduced me to my faith, to prayer and the word of God. I had to make my own choices later on in my life, but I can admit that my family was, and is still influential in my belief system.

The second source of values is in the **church/house** of worship. In this realm, man seeks to know himself better, and also tap into powers of knowledge that are greater than himself. It is acquired through reading books of spiritual inspiration, self-examination, spending time alone, journaling, serious thought time, exercise, meditation, corporate prayer, and personal private prayer. It also comes gradually over time, depending on the application.

For those who do not believe in the existence of a Higher Power, it can be difficult to grasp or agree with the spiritual aspect, but for those who have experienced this type of education, they know that it is of the highest quality and can be used to develop other abilities in the marketplace. The mental side of it gives clarity of thought and an intimate relationship with one's self.

The Spiritual dimension brings you closer to a Higher Power; what Napoleon Hill calls infinite intelligence in his book, **'Think and Grow Rich'**. He also calls this type of education, *"the sixth sense"*. The results of this type of education, when applied well, can bring about extraordinary change. This is the place of hunches, creative imagination, and innovative ideas.

Strive Masiyiwa (the founder of Econet Wireless) speaks of it when he talks about what encouraged him to pursue his court case with the government when he was applying for the Econet licence in Zimbabwe, which he won after a long legal battle. A lady of faith is said to have dreamt and told him that God confirmed that he could go ahead. Ezekiel Guti, the Founder of the Forward in Faith Church also went through the same when he had the idea of "working talents" as a way of developing his congregants to become entrepreneurs while they are fundraising for church projects.

The important thing about education is to use it, not as the end but the means to an end in your personal development. It is also essential to pick the right form of education for different circumstances. Do not be stranded.

Also, what wise leaders do is form corporations with people who specialise in various fields and are educated in different ways. They then focus on selling their vision and finding great ways to motivate their team members to work towards that vision.

In the next section, I give a summary of the three methods of acquiring education. I call it the Education Matrix. It has examples that you can use in your area of specialty and start multiplying your value even further.

The Education Matrix – Compiled By Unotida Nyoni

	Formal Education	Self –Education	Spiritual Education
Definition/ Synonyms	Pre-determined learning in formal learning institutions. Comes with a curriculum that hardly changes. Often technical and specialised.	Learning driven by the learner according to what he/she determines as the need at that time. Often general and broad in its scope.	Learning that is inspired by the principles of faith, hope, and love. Often taught in associations of faith but not limited to them.
How to acquire/ develop it	Get into a reputable institution. Get good grades. Choose program wisely. Always upgrade through further education or writing of more articles in academia. Play good politics or produce great results.	Reading books on chosen subject. Going to conferences and listening to presentations. Networking & Mentorship. Wise selection of jobs & moving when the learning experience stops.	Prayer. Personal private prayer Meditation Reading books of spiritual inspiration Self-examination. Spending time alone. Journaling. Serious thought time! Exercise. Comes gradually over time depending on application.

Results	Gets the doors opened. Usually a starting point for one's career. Gets you noticed in the job market. Makes you live through salaries and can even be an advantage for self-employed people, business owners, and investors.	Gives you additional skills in the job market. Gives the entrepreneurial edge. Gives freedom. Results are limited to the application of knowledge – Financially can be up to billions for entrepreneurs and hundreds of millions for top executives.	Has precise instruction. Great source of inspired ideas/creativity/innovation. Often taps into the future and makes the person develop new frontiers. Makes you extremely outstanding as it is rare. Serious abundance and peace of mind. Serious social impact – often to the levels of inspiring many more generations "Creative Imagination" "Hunches" Inspiration" Combined with the other 2 forms of education, it can create magic.
Demand/ Supply	There are a lot of people in this area. More than the market needs and so, there are always those who are unemployed. Serious competition. Often called the rat race.	Also a lot of people in the area but less demand than formal education.	Misunderstood by many and so very few get to tap into it, although it is readily available. Many who claim to believe in it do not exercise it fully because of doubt.

Exposure – The Second Key To Personal Excellence

During the Apartheid era in South Africa, a certain South African priest had the opportunity to relocate to the United Kingdom to study further and work there. A story is told about how he was stunned to see how well white people treated him in the UK.

At one time, as he was walking in the streets of London with his wife, he thought of asking for directions from a white policeman. Not only did he get the directions, but the policeman responded with such politeness and called them "sir" and "madam". He, later on went to work as a parish priest and had a wonderful time pastoring a church of white British citizens. It is this exposure that awakened this priest to the truth that black South Africans were living in severe oppression, and that they needed to break out of the cycle in existence. This priest is the Archbishop Desmond Tutu, who later went on to become a revolutionary spiritual and political figure in the fight against apartheid in South Africa. That, my friends, is the power of Exposure!

For our purposes, exposure is defined as coming into contact or being in a space where you can observe something different from what you are used to. It involves a change of environment. A person who has been in the rural areas of Zimbabwe might not know of the tall buildings in Harare, but once they go to Harare, they can observe the structures and learn about the city life. In the same way, a person who has grown up in urban areas has a lot to learn about life in rural areas — the best way for them to fully understand that different life is to change the environment. As you observe what happens there, the whole experience changes your views and assumptions about that changed environment. Exposure is great; it opens doors for you to see opportunities and seize them.

While I was doing my MBA at the UCT Graduate School of Business, we had an opportunity to listen to Raymond Ackerman, the ex-chairman of Pick n Pay, one of the biggest retail companies in South Africa and Africa. He told us a story about how much he learnt about the retail industry in America before he started running his own. Together with his wife, he would walk around different supermarkets in America, asking questions about how they were making money in the food industry. The exposure that he gained there made him know that something was missing in the South African industry, and he could introduce it and make money. The practice of travelling and finding out about developments in his industry has not stopped. That, my friends, is the power of exposure.

Countless other stories demonstrate the power of exposure. The Founder and ex-CEO of Debonairs Pizza, Craig Mackenzie tells a story of how he, at age twenty-three learnt about a great Pizza delivery system while he was on a gap year trip to Los Angeles, and replicated the same thing when he returned to South Africa.

In the Bible, we read about Moses, the Israelite leader who could not have had the boldness to stand before Pharaoh if he had not been exposed to free life outside Egypt. Exposure helps us to see things differently, and when we rightly choose the kind of exposure that we want in our fields, it makes us different and sets us apart from the rest.

I used to be surprised while I was working at the PWC Zimbabwe office. You could have two people with the same qualifications and years of experience, but one being promoted on account of where they have worked. Preference was given to those who had opportunities to work in different countries and markets. Those who had stayed with us in the same place would remain at the same level, because they had nothing new to offer to the team.

Where have you been in your field, and where are you going? Widen your horizons; see more things and observe the differences. You never know, your breakthrough might be coming through that difference.

Here are a few things that exposure does to you.
- It creates a new "NORMAL" in your life. When you are used to having running water in your house, you will not accept a lower "normal" of water shortages or having to travel for miles for a bucket of water.
- It widens your scope of imagination. If you observe other people performing better than what you have been exposed to, it makes you think about what else could be possible. Suddenly, a whole lot of ideas come through, and you see yourself differently.
- It opens your eyes to see opportunities for profit. Those who have gone to China and identified how affordable some of the well-sought products are, saw this as an opportunity to add a mark-up and sell them in other places around the world. The intangible asset that those people possess is "EXPOSURE". They know what is in short supply, so they look for it in other places (exposure) and then bring it to places where it's not available. Retail operations are based on this concept, but it can be applied in many other areas.

Here is what you need to do about Exposure in your field of expertise.

- Find out some of the best practices in your field. Who is doing exceptionally well in your chosen area?

- Find out how you can access information about how they do it.
- Set yourself some targets to see something different and go somewhere different, no matter how much it will cost you.
- Are there any programs that may give you that exposure for free like the Mandela Washington Fellowship or Young African Leadership Initiative program? Apply for such.
- TRAVEL and be open to living in different places, so that you can learn. Sometimes you need to see the best for you to believe that you too can become the best.
- Companies need to invest in Research and Development – and part of Research involves going to places where similar businesses are doing better or to more developed markets. This was one of the tools that the Famous Brands group used to get new ideas and change their business for the better.

  "Fanis took a team to Greece and each day, split them into smaller groups – one team had to go to Goody's, one group visited McDonald's, another Burger King, and a fourth might go to Pizza Parlour. Each evening they would meet and discuss the day's findings, the ten best ideas, and the ten worst things they had come across" (From Corner Café to JSE Giant by Carie Maas). What form of Research and Development are you doing in your business to ensure that you stay relevant and competitive? Exposure is a critical element of development in your business.

Experience – The Third Key To Personal Excellence

In one of his coaching videos, Don Moen, one of the most respected gospel musicians, tells the story of how long he worked as a keyboard player in a different band for many years. He speaks of the need for musicians to put in their time before they expect spectacular results in their careers. Years of practice in the music industry refined the man until he learnt how to compose, sing, play, lead, and produce the wonderful music that has flooded the gospel market and made him a legend in his area of speciality.

We all want to reach a certain level of excellence in our area of expertise. Many things will contribute to our greatness. Among those things, one significant one is experience. We can call it practice. It takes us being involved in that field for us to become better at what we should do. This is not to say people should not try out things in an area where they have no experience. They can, but they need to value the power of experience, so that they can make use of it.

Before a bank gives a business loan to an individual or a business, they look at the track record of that individual. How well has this person or this business done in the past? Are they able to make profits, and are they disciplined enough to pay back what they borrow? Even potential investors ask this question. Who is going to be running this business and what experience do they have in this industry? Only when they can prove that experience will they risk giving out their money. It is less risky to give money to a carpenter who wants to open a furniture manufacturing business and has been in the industry for a while than to give it to an accountant who has not been exposed to this industry.

There is power in putting in the hours, doing the drill, practising and perfecting your game. It is a fundamental principle that as time passes, you will become better at doing what you repeatedly do.

When I started driving my first car, I would watch everything I did. My friends couldn't trust that I could drive them well although I had a licence. As time passed, I became better at driving until I could change the gears without much effort or press the right pedals without having to look. I could play the radio and listen to the news or talk to my passengers without taking much care. The same principle applies to any area of expertise. We need to give ourselves time to perfect our game.

This is where getting a job in your area of interest can be a great idea for a prospective entrepreneur. It gives you the hands-on experience, the mentorship from experts in that field and the opportunity to take risks in a safer environment where you do not use your own money.

To conclude, here are some benefits of Experience.
- Experience/Practice makes perfect.
- Practice allows you to correct your mistakes and out-perform your former self.
- Experience improves confidence, which helps you push for more.
- Experience makes you a better coach and enables you to multiply your efforts by teaching others how to do it.

Here is what you need to do to improve in this area.
- Don't give up too early. There is power in compound experience. The mistakes you make now as you start will vanish as you try more.

- Push yourself to doing more in your field. Remember, you can shorten the learning period by increasing the number of hours you push in your area per day.
- Look for a profession where you can practice the things that you want, and be disciplined enough to stay there until you have mastered enough for you to go to the next level.
- Once you have learnt, there is no reason for you to stay there. Move on to a higher level of experience. Otherwise, you become redundant in your area.

Execution – The Fourth Key To Personal Execution

Execution is Action. The marketplace loves those who have mastered the habit of action. The marketplace rewards people for getting things done and shies away from people who do not deliver on their promise. The man or woman who can get things done is highly respected and highly rewarded.

The company that can deliver their promise consistently will get the customers' attention and will soon become a leader in the marketplace. The money will not flow in the direction of affirmations and promises given, but it will flow in the direction of results. Results only come when we execute the tasks that are in our promise.

I have conducted numerous interviews and have been to quite a few as well. The one thing that interviewers are looking for is the ability to get things done and deliver the results in your given job. One question that is always asked is, "What are some of your past achievements in similar jobs?" That question is asked to assess if all that you are claiming has produced results.

The first three keys to personal excellence (Education, Experience, and Exposure) will not multiply our value if you are not taking action.

Execution separates the excellent from the average. Those who achieve excellent results have mastered the habit of executing their tasks consistently, while those who are average have mastered the art of giving excuses for why things could not be done. The more the excuses we have in our bag, the fewer results we will have, and the lower the value we will have in the marketplace.

The man or woman of action respects doing things "NOW", while the average earner always uses words like "tomorrow or later". The present is a friend of great executors while the future is the best friend to those who deliver on their promise.

So, how do we get to that place where execution becomes our habit? How do we get to a place where we are known more for what we do than what we say? How do we get to the place where we have something to show for the work that we regularly do? Here are a few simple steps that will get us going.

1. **Break big tasks into smaller, manageable tasks.** When a task looks big, it can be demotivating, but when you break it down into smaller steps, you start seeing that it can be accomplished. A journey of a thousand miles begins with a single step. When you start working on the first task, and you finish it, you start building the confidence to the next.

   The idea of writing this book had been in my mind for a while, but I could never start, because I had a picture of a full book in my head. After going to a writing seminar, one of my well-respected mentors and authors told us that it is easier to write blogs than it is to write a book. His first book was a combination of the blogs that he had written. That gave me a place to start. The next week, I gathered the courage to write my first article and publish it on LinkedIn. That is precisely how the book started. The first article led to weekly articles that gave me the momentum to continue with the rest of my book.

   The feeling of accomplishment came from completing the first blog, and it gave me the strength to keep going. What is it that you are thinking of doing? Can you break it down and do it in smaller tasks? Write down those smaller tasks and begin to do something about it.

2. **Set deadlines for your tasks.** You must give yourself a timeline for the things that you want to do. I find that useful, primarily when I work with a team. I can decide on a deadline for my tasks and then share that with my team. The moment a deadline is set, written down, and shared with others, the mind begins to focus on getting that task done. After proposing to my wife, Ellen, in December 2016, I had to share my plans with her on when I would be ready to meet with her family to pay lobola (dowry). The moment I told her the date that I would be prepared and she shared that with her aunt, everything around me had to change. With not much money saved, I knew that I now had to increase my monthly savings, reduce my spending and prepare myself for that tremendous day. I could tell that setting a deadline for myself was a crucial part of changing how I worked.

Companies can do the same when they are about to release a new product. They give a date to the market and then start working towards releasing the product on that given date. The moment that date is set, a promise is delivered and therefore has to be met. It creates a sense of urgency for that task, and thus teams begin to focus on that particular task, so that they meet the promise. Tasks that do not have deadlines are easy to leave out, but when a timeframe is set, the mind is empowered to start working on how to get the task done.

3. **Prioritise.** Tasks can be described in terms of two main categories. These are the levels of **importance,** and **urgency.** Important tasks are those that are essential for our wellbeing. Spending family time, for example, is critical to any relationship. Once you no longer spend time communicating with each other, it is easy

to lose each other. For a business, growing your client base or managing your cash-flow is an essential role for survival of the business, as the business depends on it.

When we measure how urgent a task is, we are asking how much time that task can wait before it can be done. Every task usually has a deadline by which it must be done. Once that deadline passes, an opportunity is missed, or there is a penalty that comes with it that hurts the progress of the project at hand. So, tasks are classified as urgent or not urgent. The 34th president of the United States of America, Dwight D. Eisenhower wanted to simplify time management for his team so much that he created a matrix that has now become known as the Eisenhower's principle/matrix. See the diagram below.

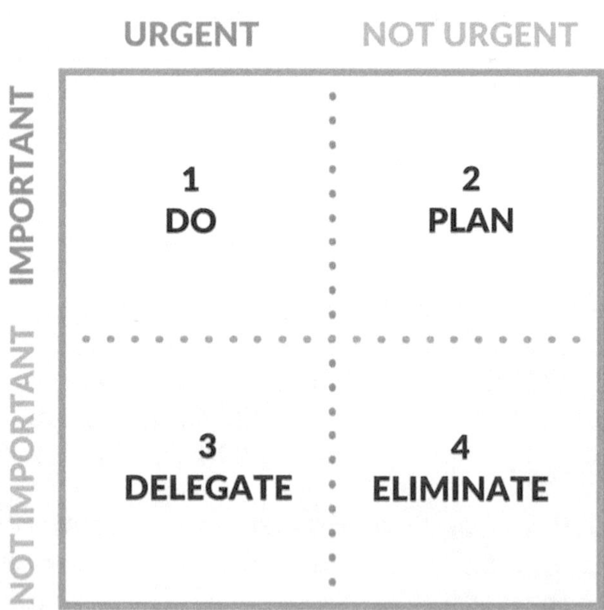

The matrix has four boxes, which represent the different combinations of the two categories explained above. In box one are Urgent and Important tasks. These tasks must be done immediately, because leaving them will hinder our progress in a big way. The second box is Important but Not Urgent. These tasks must be planned for and executed before they become too urgent. That is the place that most of our time should be spent. A good time manager will have few urgent and essential things to do because they would have managed to complete the tasks before they become urgent.

The third set of tasks are Urgent but Not Important. If you have a team to work with, these are the tasks that you delegate so that you focus on more essential tasks. As a leader or manager, you should focus on the tasks that have a significant effect on your results. The last set of tasks are Not Urgent, and they are not necessary. These must be left out entirely as they do not affect your results.

4. **Surround yourself with people who are achieving the same results that you desire.** Whatever you want to do in your life, there is someone else who has already done it. Granted, you may want to do it differently, but some have travelled a similar path. Get to know who they are and how they have accomplished those great things.

An aspiring author should surround himself with accomplished and aspiring authors, too. If there is an association of book writers near you, join that group and listen to what they had to go through for them to be well accomplished. If you want to be a great speaker, join an association of people that want to perfect their speaking. If you want to be a great inventor, find associations that you can join where inventors meet. If there are no physical meetings taking place in your area, then join an online platform that has people who are on that same journey. In this era of the internet, you can have a group for almost anything that you want in life. If there are no groups available, then start one and ask people to join. Invite a speaker to come and coach you or share their story. That way, you get the idea.

Many of my colleagues at JCI have started their businesses. When I ask them why they started on that path, they always say that there was some peer pressure for them to start something. One senator told me that he went to an international conference and when he met with other members, almost all of them were running their own companies.

Now, being an aspiring entrepreneur, full of excuses of why he needed to wait, he found himself thinking, "If these young people can do it, what's my excuse?" It is that year that he decided that he was going to start something and not wait any longer. Now he runs a successful IT consulting company that employs ten people. Had he not gone to that conference and interacted with other young people who have similar dreams and passions, he might have kept his excuses and would have never started his company.

5. **Never wait for conditions to be perfect before you can start.** Our minds work in such a way that we look for the path of least resistance. We want to do the least work and get the most results. As a result, we find ourselves looking for that path of least resistance. However, months can pass while we are still looking for that easy path, and sometimes it never comes.

The truth of the matter is that conditions will never be perfect for you to start. There will always be something missing. The best thing you can do is to start where you are, with what you have, and figure out the rest later. Many things would have stopped me from pursuing my MBA at the University of Cape Town. Firstly, I did not have the money to go onto the program. Secondly, I had no scholarship. I also did not know anyone in

Cape Town, and so I had no place to stay. Nevertheless, where there is a will, there is a way.

The first thing I did was to look at the requirements of the program, and when I figured that I had to write GMAT exams, I registered for those. I did not have funds for the fees, but I certainly had enough for GMAT exams. Next, I had to find the GMAT book and study. The best learning method for me is always the classroom, but no place offered such classes, so I had to rely on YouTube videos. I downloaded as many and started studying. Next, I went for the exam and wrote my first exam. That did not go too well, but I still went on for the second time.

Meanwhile, I was completing the rest of my application. On my second attempt, the results were better, and so I sent those to the admissions team. A few weeks later, I had been admitted to the program. The joy I felt when that happened is something I couldn't even explain. One would have thought that I had all the money for the program. My mentors who had done similar programs before rejoiced with me and encouraged me to start applying for scholarships or at least, look for sources of funding, just for the deposit. After getting deposit funds from friends, it was time to get half the fees. I had only applied for a loan intending to buy a car, and the funds came right at the time when I needed to pay for my fees. That's how the first half was paid, and a door was created for the program to start.

At the time of writing this book, I was still paying off loans and balances, but the program was done. Had I waited for conditions to be perfect before I started, I would not have completed the program. There were many reasons why I could not do it, but through the help of friends, family, and mentors, I managed to find reasons for getting onto the program. Just the little doors that opened along the way were good enough for me to step in and figure out the rest later.

6. **Do not rely on your feelings or emotions when deciding to take action.** The people who have mastered the art of executing tasks well know that their opinions are not to be trusted when getting things done. Ellen, my wife, is one of the smartest people I know. She always wants her house to be super clean no matter what the circumstances are. I, on the other hand, am still learning to at least maintain her standard so that we are always in good books☺. The one thing I have learnt from her when it comes to keeping the house clean is that as soon as we return from work, she identifies one thing that's not clean in the house and before she decides to take a seat, she goes ahead and cleans that part of the house.

I suppose she has been doing that for a long time now that it is part of her habit, and slowly (I repeat, slowly) becoming mine too. She may be feeling tired, but as soon as she gets into the house, it's as if the dirt that she sees motivates her to at least do something before she rewards herself with a bit of time to relax.

Imagine if we could take that approach in every little thing that we do, where we do not wait to feel good to do good. That's how we get things done.

PART 4 – REVOLUTIONISE YOUR MINDSET

The Power Of Keeping A Positive Mental Attitude

THROUGH OBSERVATION, I have learnt that it is difficult to travel on the success path without keeping a positive mental attitude. All successful people that I have met have this attribute. It is the one thing that you see in them as they walk, and you hear from them as they speak.

I used to work for an entrepreneur who always believed that "The Man above was always good to him". He believed it so much that he would act and make decisions in his company with the firm belief that he would be well taken care of. He believed that tomorrow would be better; that many opportunities were waiting for him and his company in the future. For the three years that I worked with him, I could see how much of what he believed and said was coming to life.

Despite all hardship he faced in his entrepreneurship journey, he opened new branches for his business every year. Every year, he won an award, or his business received some recognition that propelled it further. His language never changed, regardless of all the challenges he faced. As the Chief Financial Officer in the organisation, I could see the reality in the numbers, but he was reading his reality from a different source. He was creating the numbers in his head, and they were coming to life in our financial statements. When he made a decision and spoke about the desired outcome, one could tell that every fibre of his being believed what he was saying. Being around him would leave you with no choice but to believe that, too, and start working towards the vision that had been released.

One of the things I admired about this entrepreneur was how much he could take advantage of the opportunities that came his way. His positive mental attitude could make him turn the minimal resources that he had into much more significant results. Through his positive mental attitude, I saw him conquering and multiplying the little that he had, daily. I saw how he fought negativity. Negativity was not an option in his mind. He had a way of chasing it away and attracting the positivity back into his life, no matter what. He also protected his company from that negativity in the way that he chose his team members.

Luvuyo Rani is a social entrepreneur, the Co-Founder and Managing Director of Silulo Ulutho Technologies. His company has impacted over 35 000 students from the South African townships, and assisted them in securing jobs and opening up their minds. He has championed the IT revolution in the S.A townships. The company now has more than 42 branches and has empowered so many employees that they have become franchise owners in his business. When you hear the story of how the company started, you can see the maintenance of a positive mental attitude throughout the time. You can sense his firm belief that everything is going to be alright.

Another guru that I deeply respect is Professor Ezekiel Handinawangu Guti, the Founder of Forward In Faith Ministries International. Having been a beneficiary of his ministry from when I was a little boy, I have made observations, read many stories and witnessed many things happening around him. His ministry is now in more than 120 countries, with more than 5000 pastors and a membership that goes into the millions. The one attribute that is almost tangible in his walk is that of a positive mental attitude, also expressed as faith. His eyes see more than what the natural eye looks at. When he was starting in ministry, he believed that his ministry was going to be bigger than the

Roman Catholic Church. Here was an African man, with little education, coming from an impoverished background, but who believed that everything was going to be alright. He believed that God was on his side and was backing him all the way.

When you look at some of the decisions that he makes and some of the exploits he works out in ministry, you have this sense that he knows in his heart of hearts that everything is going to be alright, that a more significant force is in charge and has assured him that the unseen promise is going to come to pass. When he encounters obstacles, they don't become his reality, because he carries the reality in his head.

In 2011, I came across another pastor who had developed this attribute to such an extent that I couldn't wait to talk to him after I heard him speak. He had just written his first book called **'Dream Big and Make It Happen'**, and was making a presentation at my friend's book launch. Without much hesitation, I bought his audiobook, and when I got home, I started listening to it. Here was a man who believed in the power of big dreams, and was willing to back that up with everything that he had.

As I listened to that audio recording repeatedly, I decided to make him a part of my network, invited him to preach at our youth group, and started following him and acquiring mentorship from him at every point that I could. The same attribute that I saw from Luvuyo and Professor Guti were visible to me. You could hear it in his words, and see it in his actions. He walked with the confidence that Heaven and all its angels were on his side. You could even sense it when you attended his church. There was a song that the team there used to sing that I cannot forget to this day. It said, "Greater things are still to come, greater things are still to be done in this city."

In April 2016, this very same pastor started something that changed the face of the civic movement in Zimbabwe. He stood up and spoke truth to power in a way that the powerful government became confused and shaken. One man spoke about the reality of corruption, lack of governance, and concern for human life in a way that captured the hearts of the masses of Zimbabwe and gave them hope and courage. The whole government did not know what to do with him, such that its leaders tried to eliminate him, but throughout, he kept the positive mental attitude that told him that tomorrow was going to be better. From speaking to him, it was clear that he had not lost the same attribute that I have been talking about in this chapter. A firm belief that The Man above is on his side; and that's all that matters for a man who is on a mission. The "greater things" had started unfolding.

I could go on and on about many other people that have moved mountains, but what I know is that this attribute is critical if one is to achieve anything worthwhile in life. You and I have to embrace it if we are to fulfil our calling and purpose in our generation. You can trace this in all great men and women of our time, and if you look carefully, you will notice that this was the driving force that kept them sane and focused on a higher purpose. The question is, will you embrace this, and if so, how will you do it? Let's discuss this in the coming principle. We will call this positive mental attitude by other names like "faith".

The Disorganised Nature Of Faith

I will use the three men that I talked about in the previous chapter to explain how a positive mental attitude can be embraced and cultivated for your good. I will also add personal examples and those of other people that I have witnessed, so that it becomes clearer as we go.

Firstly, you need to be fully convinced of your inner truth and vision more than you are convinced of what you can see outside. Until that becomes true in your life, you will not push your conviction and truth into existence confidently. When challenges come, the reality outside will speak louder than your inner truth and vision. If the outside reality is louder and more convincing, you will do what most people do, and that is called giving up. Your inner truth and vision will become a lie, swallowed by the truth and reality that you have faced outside.

In the early chapters of this book, I mentioned the story of David and Goliath. In David's head existed a different inner reality than what could be seen by the physical eye. He believed in his heart that with God on his side, he could conquer a troop and leap over a high wall. He had seen this, tested it, and that had become his reality. To the naked, untrained eye, this was pure madness. Even the King thought that this was a joke. This is how crazy it can get.

What do you think was going on in Pastor Evan Mawarire's head as he was walking daily with his flag and posting videos of peaceful protests? The inner reality that was bigger than the Goliath all Zimbabweans were facing had overtaken his mind and consumed it. It was a reality of what could be, that convinced him to start making a move.

Prof Ezekiel Guti is known for going into nations without any idea of where he is going to sleep or who is going to receive him when he goes to preach the Word in that nation for the first time. The inner reality that God is with him and he is a messenger of the Gospel has become the bigger reality than the thought that he might not reach a place to sleep, or funds to sustain him in that nation. That's what keeps him going.

In the same way, I witnessed new branches being established at Silulo with Luvuyo Rani's work. Together with his brother Lonwabo and sister-in-law Nandipha, they started talking about 100 new branches in the country when they only had 26. You would think that this was a scientifically proven number, but after talking to them, you realised that it was a reality that came from within and not from without. That number drove their actions and the activities of the entire organisation. In no time, inquiries of new branches and resources to establish them started coming.

Do you see how disorganised this positive mental attitude is? Do you see how crazy it can get? Do you see how it cannot be taught in school? Hahahaha! You and I have to find our inner vision truth and follow it, too.

I could say the same thing about some of my heroes in the arts industry. Mr Thato Sikwane's story has similar truths. Born in Botswana to a lawyer and government official, one would have thought that Thato's path would be traditional. Here was a young man who had his path defined, being taken to great schools for him to acquire a formal education that would land him into a great job, so his father hoped.

The young man, however, was consumed by a passion for music that became a big reality for him. It consumed his hobbies and at some point, made him meet other young people who were doing great exploits in a neighbouring country. When the reality of becoming a great DJ came into Thato's mind, and he saw it through the inner eye, it became so real that he decided to quit school and follow his dream in South Africa. With no job offer, he went for interviews with the hope that he could get his first gig and try out his passion/hobby and hopefully make a life out of it. Yes, Mr Sikwane tried it out, worked his way up in the industry of his passion and became an award-winning and influential legend. My wife and I listen to him every morning on our way to work. His industry name is DJ Fresh, a legend whose inner dream pushed him to create more than it could be easily seen outside. He is now a renowned music producer, entrepreneur, radio & television producer, philanthropist, and much more.

The same story could be told of Mr Nkosinathi Innocent Maphumulo, but I digress now. Let's talk about him later when we talk about the second ingredient to having a great positive mental attitude.

Get Used To Being Criticised, Misunderstood And Isolated And Still Be Okay

Now, because of the very nature of a positive mental attitude (PMA) or faith, you will face opposition. As explained in the above principle, it is crazy and abnormal. It comes from an inner vision, an inner conviction that only the recipient can see. It is a gift from the universe, which comes in the form of a seed of thought, and given the right conditions, that thought becomes a consuming obsession and convinces the recipient that this is a new reality. Once the recipient believes in the reality of this new possibility and starts bringing it into life, there will be serious resistance. Ninety per cent of that resistance will not come from circumstances; it will come from the people around, because this new concept/thought/idea will not be a common one.

Think about how the Wright brothers were criticised, laughed at and mocked for trying to find a way for humans to fly into the sky. The very thought of flying during their time was thought of as madness. There is something about us as human beings that makes us believe in what we have seen and tested more than anything else. We forget that at some point, we were also just an idea, a thought, a cell that did not have life in it. It is this very nature that makes us look at anything different from what we have understood and known, as absurd and crazy, and that's where our criticism emanates.

Do you remember the crazy man I told you about in the last chapter – Pastor Evan Mawarire? When you watch the first video that he posted, the one that made him known as Founder of the **'This Flag Movement'**? You will find that the comments that came with that video were not encouraging. Of course, what he said resonated with what many Zimbabweans were feeling about their government and country at that time, but their reality at that time opposed the thinking that this man had introduced. The reality was that the regime that was in power was ruthless and merciless. Many people who had taken this path had gone missing, and many who had tried to resist the government and to question their authority had ended up in damming silence. So those who cared for him and their own lives began to criticise and silence him. Others called him an agent of the very evil system that he was opposing. Just reading a page of comments on some of the videos that he posted would make one think that he would give up the next day. That faith, that positive mental attitude, that inner conviction in him was stronger, louder than these voices. Instead of shutting up, he went on posting more videos and started calling other people to join him in the call to get the government to account for what they were doing in the country.

Day by day, the movement grew, and it gave birth to more movements, and the voices of the voiceless citizens became more audible to the government and the international community. If he had just listened to the opposing voices that told him to keep quiet and go on doing his regular duties as a pastor, the new concept or idea he had would have died a natural death.

In the same way, Luvuyo Rani was told by many of his colleagues that he was crazy when he quit his job and started selling computers from the boot of his car. In his mind, he had seen it and had been convinced that computers were going to be the future of education and therefore, there was room for him to make a difference in that industry. Although it wasn't clear how this was going to happen, he knew that this was going to be his new path.

Criticism can get so bad and personal that it can change you if you are not careful. In the African community, when people see someone making progress that's out of the usual, they even go on to ascribe the achievements to some evil forces and "muti". Luvuyo also faced such criticism, but once again, his inner conviction was stronger than the words that he received from outside, so it couldn't stop him. It was only after some time that the community started seeing the positive results that were coming out of his company that they started recognising him in a big way.

Apostle Ezekiel Guti went through the same things. The amount of criticism that he faced as a black African man trying to start a church in an industry/sector that had mostly mainline churches that had begun in the Western countries was HUGE. Yet he had received this concept/thought/idea that he was to be a father of many nations, and that his church would be bigger than the Catholic Church. When miracles started taking place in the church, some people said he was using evil powers. However, that did not stop him. It could have stopped him if he had taken it to heart, but the vision that he had was a bigger reality than the forces of criticism.

Now, how ready are you to be criticised? How prepared are you to be misunderstood? How ready are you to be lonely in your journey? At some point, you have to believe that you are the majority in your quest for greatness. As one of my mentors put it, you have to believe that the opinion that matters the most is yours, and shake off that criticism as you move into what you believe you have been called to do.

The Story Of Alice The Frog

A story is told about some frogs that had come across a massive wall in their journey to find water. It was a matter of survival as the frogs could only find water on the other side of the wall. There were mixed views on the team, though. Some frogs did not think it was a good idea to try and climb that wall, because it was too high for the tired team of frogs.

"By the time we get there, we would be dead. Let's find another route and go in different direction, guys."

Some frogs were determined, and so they started climbing. The frogs that were opposing this move began shouting at the frogs that were trying to climb up the big wall.

"Why are you wasting our time and energy, guys? We need to be reserving it for a different path."

As these words were being shouted into the ears of the climbing frogs, some frogs gave up and returned to the ground. In fact, after several hours, all the frogs gave up climbing, so that they could look for a different path, or be ready to die with the rest of the team.

All, except one frog, Alice, who kept climbing up for as long as it took until she reached the top of the wall. As Alice the top, she looked excited because she could now see the dam that the team had been looking for. It was only when at the top of the wall that the rest of the team was motivated to climb, too. She had led the team through her determination to go in spite of what was other doubting frogs said.

When the rest of the team tried to ask Alice about what had inspired her to keep going, they discovered that she was deaf. She had lost her sense of hearing during the journey. So while all the other frogs were shouting, she wasn't discouraged by it, she kept going because she heard none of it. She could not hear what led the team to the dam where they could live to see another day.

Sometimes we need to put some earplugs into our ears and keep moving until we reach our destination. In the journey of success, listening to the opinions of those who have not even walked the journey you are about to start will keep you in stagnation. Go for what you believe you have been called to do, trust yourself and God to take you there. Encourage yourself and tell yourself how much you are the apple of God's eye. Know that it only takes you and the help of "The Man above" to move the mountains of poverty in your township. Others will join you when you get to the top, but for now, get used to walking in your lonely path.

Developing An Entrepreneurial Mindset

As we live in this life, we should know that we have everything we need for us to survive in the world. I was sitting in church during our Easter conference, and the preacher said something that blew my mind. He said that in the story of creation, we see that God first created the environment before he put the creatures that were to live in the background. Before the fish were created, the oceans and the seas were brought into existence. Before the animals that live on the ground were created, the ground was also created.

In the same way, before human beings were created, the environment that is conducive for him to not only survive but thrive was also created. Now, this revelation made me think hard about my life. If everything conducive for my thriving is around me, then I must find what is in my environment that can make me thrive. If I fail to succeed, then it's not because of the lack of resources, but because of my inability to see the opportunities around me that enable me to thrive.

That ability to see and take advantage of opportunities around us and strengths within us is what I call the entrepreneurial mindset. A cheetah, by nature, is a fast-running animal. It is endowed with speed as its survival advantage. When a cheetah is hungry, and it needs to feed, it looks around the area for prey that is usually slower than it is, and takes advantage of that opportunity. That's what makes it live for another day. It means that the cheetah has a simple ability to see an opportunity before it and use its strength to take advantage of it.

Now, how do we, as human beings, identify our opportunities and take advantage of them? How do we get to know about our inner abilities? How do we look around for opportunities? How do we grow those opportunities to such an extent that we can live prosperous lives from now going forward? How do we do it in such a way that we leave an inheritance for our children and grandchildren? Here are a few thoughts that take us to that position.

- Read/listen to the news for updates of what is happening in the world. This sounds simple, but it is profound, too. A person who is looking for a job opportunity has to look for a job in a place where job givers reveal what jobs they are offering in the market. Unless you develop the habit of searching, hearing, and listening, your chances of getting hold of that information about jobs are reduced. The same applies to your business. You will know about opportunities in your area if you keep your ears on the ground.

- Listen to the people around you. Every day, people talk about the challenges they are facing in their lives. You need to know that every problem that is presented to you presents an equal opportunity for value creation and therefore, for business/solution creation. A high crime rate in an area increases the need for security services. A high unemployment rate increases the need for job creators and employment agencies, too. We could go on and on. Facebook, Twitter, Snapchat and many other social media platforms were created to fulfil a human need to connect. Many other requirements are presented to us every day, and some have always been there. Here are a few examples of human needs. Needs for:
    - Housing/Shelter
    - Financial security
    - Physical security
    - Love
    - Recognition
    - Leaving a legacy
    - Clothing
    - Food
    - Health

Education

- o Connection
- o Sex
- o Hope
- o Faith and purpose
- o Power
- o Travel
- o Happiness (Entertainment)
- o Rest
- o Peace
- o Justice
- o Reconciliation

We could go on and on, but as you can see, these are industries, and they are all based on human needs. What needs can you see in your area and what role can you play to meet those needs? Therein lies your survival, therein lies your opportunity to thrive. We only really succeed when we meet the needs of other people. That's how we develop our happiness, health, and wealth. It is through service. Those who devise the best methods of serving as many people usually thrive in the best way.

- Observe the people around you. It is one thing to listen to the people around you. It is another thing to observe them. When you listen to people, they will tell you what they think their needs are, but when you observe them, you will also pick up the requirements that they are not saying at all. Remember what Steve Jobs said, *"People don't know what they want until you show it to them."* Some of the services that we are now using daily were not in existence before. When they were presented to the human family, we loved them, embraced them, and now we cannot do without them. Take the telephone, or better still, the mobile phone. The creator of the mobile telephone realised through observation that it was stressful for people to be confined to one place where they could take their telephone calls from, and thus started looking for ways to create the mobile phone as it made things more convenient.

As we speak right now, some companies are investigating how we can increase the battery life of the phones that we use or how we can use battery-less phones. Why? Because through observation, you can tell that people would appreciate the convenience of not having to struggle with power. That's what throws us into the realm of innovation.

What is the next innovation that will make life easier for people? When you start thinking like this in your industry, life gets exciting, and you can begin creating products/services that will serve the people while you make money.

- Increase your exposure. Many businesses have been created based on this very concept alone. A person travels to a different place and discovers that there is something in that country that is or could be of high demand in their country, then devises a way to get that product/service back to their country. Pick n Pay's whole competitive advantage in its formative days was based on the knowledge that Raymond Ackerman had acquired through researching the supermarket industry in the USA. He had used his time and energy to see what was provided in advanced markets, took it back home, and tailored it to the South African needs. I did emphasise the value of exposure in a separate part of this book, so please feel free to go to that section for more.

- See what is not there and imagine what could be done to make it come to life. Many of the things that we see today were not there before. The light bulb that we see today was not there at some point. Electricity too, and many other human inventions that have solved human challenges and problems. As we all know, human challenges have not yet stopped anywhere in the world. Every country has its challenges, and they need solutions. Some of the solutions can come through exposure, as I mentioned above, but some of the answers are not yet available to humankind. We need to research and experiment with different kinds of possibilities for us to come up with a solution. This is a much more superior realm for wealth creation than many other ways because the person with the first advantage usually protects that advantage.

- Listen to yourself. Now, this is where it gets interesting. You have been designed in such a way that there are things that arouse a specific reaction in you. Some things make you feel happy, sad, angry, proud, and the list goes on. When you can read into these things and catch yourself while you are caught up in that emotion, therein lies an opportunity for you. What am I saying? Let's take anger, for example. If you find yourself in situations where you get angry when others are mistreated, there lies a passion for **"advocacy"**, and that's a whole industry on its own. It's a seed that's telling you that you could be in that position as an activist or lawyer, or more options in that industry. In other words, your anger becomes an indicator of where you are best placed to serve. It shows the area where you have the most energy to solve problems, and thus create value. It shows the area where you have **"passion"**. Remember the SHAPE we talked about in self-discovery. This personal knowledge and discovery will help you choose among the many areas of focus.
- Invest time in upgrading your skills and knowledge around the area/s that you have identified, so that you see where you can best serve the people. This has been covered in the Education principle.

- Join associations of people who have the same desire to solve problems in your area of interest. This is critical. Farmers create farmer's unions to share best practices. Accountants have the same kind of organisations. So do professional speakers. Associations are a great way for you to acquire knowledge and even get business. I love the South African saying that goes, "Uzoy'thola kanjani uhlel'ekhoneni" (How are you going to get it while you are sitting in the corner). If you don't join associations where people can see you, how are you going to be noticed? If you don't come out and advertise your services and say, "this is what I am doing now", who will know that you are providing the services or products that you are providing?

- There is an ancient scripture that says, *"No one lights a lamp and puts it in a place where it will be hidden, or under a bowl. Instead, they put it on its stand, so that those who come in may see the light."* Makes so much sense, right? You are the light, endowed with gifts and strengths that are meant to make this world a better place for all of us. If you are hiding somewhere and not coming out, though, you will burn the fuel in the light for no cause. You will run out of your time here on earth without having an impact in the world.

- Dream big! This is important. The dream that you have should be more significant than yourself. This is the only way you can be motivated to do more. Several material has been written about this, but let me put a different angle to it. Whereas most of the messages we hear are about dreaming big in terms of the money and achievements that we will make, I would like to challenge you to dream of bigger solutions. Wealth is only a result of big solutions that have been given out to the people. So, instead of thinking about supplying your church with your products/services, think about how you can reach out to a bigger market.

Instead of thinking about solving legal problems for your small firm, think about how you can solve more problems in your country. An entrepreneurial mindset is always thinking of bigger and better solutions.

When I started working at Silulo, the company only had 25 stores. What I remember clearly at that time is that the owners of that social enterprise were already thinking and working towards establishing 100 stores. That was always the target. They were only in two provinces at the time, but the big vision was to be in all nine provinces of the country within five years. It's been quite some time now, but they are now reaching 50% of the goal that they were working towards. The whole management team was sure that this was what needed to happen.

Here's the thing. A bigger dream gives you a reason to wake up in the morning. A bigger dream motivates your team as well. A bigger dream makes you look in and outside yourself for possible solutions.

Ultimately, bigger dreams make us become better people, in spite of whether we achieve them or not.

So yes, go ahead and dare to dream big!

PART 5 – DEVELOP YOUR

ENTREPRENEURIAL HABITS

NOW THAT WE know the mindset of the entrepreneur, we can go into the entrepreneurial behaviour. It is not a mistake that we have placed the topics in this order. The mindset comes first before the behaviours show. That is precisely the concept that the great author, Napoleon Hill was saying in the book '**Think and Grow Rich'**. His emphasis was on the mindset that transforms ideas into riches. I would encourage you to get hold of that book and go through it if you haven't done so already.

Now, after the mind is set in a certain way of thinking (the entrepreneurial mindset), we need to let the mind drive us into action. I have tried to make this simple, so that we could break down the somewhat seemingly complex matters of entrepreneurship into simplified language, and hopefully, this will add something that will drive you towards your dream and purpose. Here are the five behaviours that I have noticed in many successful entrepreneurs and leaders that I have worked and associated with in the past thirteen years.

Write It Down

The late Dr Steve Covey understood and powerfully explained this concept. In his book, **'The Seven Habits of Highly Effective People'**, he points out the ability to *"begin with the end in mind"* as one of the seven habits. He points out how important it is to first have creations in the mind before they come into existence. When we look at it clearly, this is the same principle that the people in the construction industry use. They do not erect a building before the plan has been completed and approved. The plan is written on paper, showing all the rooms and what each of the rooms will be used for. Before the foundation is even put up, the planners know that there is going to be a study, a kitchen and a bathroom. If you ask them what kind of bathroom it is, they can show you the type of facilities that are going to be in the bathroom. Is it going to have a normal bathtub and a shower, or is it going to have a jacuzzi? That's the kind of detailed information that the plan can give you. This practice is critical in life, and it is one of the most vital entrepreneurial behaviours. Here are some ideas on how you can create your first creations.

- Keep a journal. A journal is a special book where your thoughts, reflections, and reactions to circumstances are written down. It is a personal asset that helps capture the thoughts that go through your mind. Good ideas need a place where they can be stored. Good thoughts also need to be stored in a place where they can be revisited and analysed for your benefit. As I have said, you are free to keep a manual one or even one on your computer or phone as long as it is safe and it can be easily referred to. Here's why it is essential to keep and update your journal.
    - A journal offers an effective way to figure it all out. In other words, writing is a fantastic problem-solving tool.
    Sometimes we go through challenges, and they can become overwhelming in our minds. There is

something magical about writing it down. In the process of writing it all out, you start to figure out how to make it work. Writing allows us to ponder our situations objectively. When we describe a problem in our minds, our imagination tends to send distorted information about how things are. When we write, however, we become more factual, objective, accurate, and realistic. As we re-read what we have written, we see a new picture of the situation in our minds, which replaces the distorted picture that we had.

- A journal allows you to capture good ideas. You get to write your plans down. You should understand that thoughts visit your mind all the time. and they are not permanent. Constructive thoughts or ideas need to be respected for them to start taking life. They need to get their first form of life somewhere, and usually, a pen and a paper does the trick. I do this all the time, and I make sure that I buy a journal every year. In these exciting times we are in, ideas can be stored in many places - computers, phones, tablets, and physical books. You can practically write anywhere.

Develop the habit of writing those thoughts and ideas when they visit your mind. The idea could come through at night, and all you have to do is grab a phone, write the thought so that it doesn't escape before it gains life.

One of my pastors, who is also an author and musician used to tell us that he can get a tune of a new song at night. After that, he wakes up and records one verse on his phone. The next morning, he can start working on the song, because he has stored it somewhere. He uses the same principle in writing books. Once an idea hits the mind, he wakes up and writes a few notes so that the next day, he can start working on that idea.

We all have our "aha" moments that we get when we are working. The idea is to receive that gift of thought, that idea, and give it life by writing it down. Studies have shown that when something is written down, it is more likely to stick into your memory than when it's just a thought that has visited your mind.

- Stored ideas can be brought together to form new ideas. When we can gather enough ideas from different sources in any area of life, we can form a solid block of a whole new life. This is why we should never get tired of having new ideas and thoughts about our area of passion, business, calling, and purpose. It's as if these ideas have a way of talking to each other and bringing out new outcomes. Remember that "*any positive change which occurs within you will always ultimately manifest itself in a positive result outside of you*" (Jim Rohn).

The gathering of great ideas in your head is a positive change in your head, and the greater ideas come in, the better the person you become. Imagine the power of ideas that are carefully constructed and stuck in your head through the effort of writing. It multiplies the power of the idea, so keep a journal, my friend.

- A journal allows you to review your ideas whenever you want to do so. It is a great practice to go through your journals once in a while and record some of the things you have been writing.
- A journal reveals our innermost feelings. If you use the journal to record what has happened and reflect on events that take place, you will also write about how what happened made you feel.

The better we become at describing what goes on around us, the better we will understand some of the conflict and turmoil taking place within us. You will begin to see some trends that inform you how you think, what drives your feelings, and which people/environments excite you and make you grow.

- A journal gives you a chance to talk to yourself. I know that sounds a little weird, but it is healthy for you to speak to yourself. Writing a journal is one of the most effective ways of developing communication skills. You become better at explaining what you feel to yourself, and that makes you express your feelings to others, and in return, you can understand what others are saying to you.

Cast And Sell Your Vision

Now, once you begin the practice of playing around with good ideas and writing them down, you would have started casting the vision. It will be taking form in your mind. The next thing that needs to happen to bring the vision to life is to communicate it well to all the people that are necessary for it to come to pass. In the business world, they call them stakeholders.

Such are parties that have an interest in your activities in one way or the other. In my research, I have observed that many great leaders and entrepreneurs can sell their vision so well that people can buy into it and help them achieve their dreams. The bigger the success of the individual, the better they have become at selling. We may not realise it, but, we are selling every day. When we try and convince our baby to eat vegetables even if they don't like it, we are selling the benefits of vegetables to them. We are trying to convince them that this is the best way to go. At work, our delivery of work and how we communicate to colleagues is a part of selling.

So usually when people talk about sales, they picture the man on the street trying to sell newspapers or the salesman in the clothing store trying to convince a customer to buy that blue shirt, and encouraging him to take a little bit more so that he can meet his sales target.

While this is a part of sales, it's not the rest of it. There is a whole thought and practice process that goes in before the closing of the sale. It is that process that we want to go through and look at how we can start practising this area of our life until it becomes a habit.

Below are the several practices that extremely great salespeople have. The great thing is that we can all learn to be great, and we can all improve in this area until we become formidable brands in the marketplace. So here it is:

- **Great salespeople invest in building their confidence in themselves and in what they have to offer.** Here is the thing. Customers don't buy services or products.

They buy people. What do I mean by that? I mean we could have the same products with different brand names, and the thing that will make the difference in the customer's mind is the difference the people bring behind each brand. Are the people behind the brand able to communicate the value of their product/service to such an extent that the product becomes something the customer must have? They have both self-confidence and product confidence. That is what makes the difference.

Now, here is how self-confidence and product confidence is developed. They are developed by the knowledge that you have about what makes you unique and what makes the product/service that you are offering unique. The moment you are equipped with that knowledge, you become confident of getting out to the marketplace and sell your brand and your products. In the same way, confidence is diminished whenever we see ourselves as people who have nothing different to offer to the marketplace.

It is, therefore, your job to sit down and study what makes you unique. The truth is that you have something that makes you unique and a special touch that differentiates you from others. However, unless you know it, you will always sell yourself short. Once you have that knowledge, however, you will work on developing that special uniqueness, because that is what will build your value. Refer to the topic about your SHAPE, because that is what defines who you are.

Product/service confidence is what they call your Unique Selling Proposition (USP) in the marketing and sales language. You need to develop confidence in what you are offering to the market, so that the market can accept and buy what you have. The fact is that what you have is already unique, but if you don't know what makes it special, then your confidence in the product/service goes down, and the marketplace can pick it up. It is the brands that always stand out that we repeatedly buy.

Take the example of Sprite. Sprite has been presented to the marketplace as a thirst quencher. That has been the unique selling point of that fizzy drink. Now, there could be many other drinks that do the same, but the Sprite brand stands out in that area because that's how it has always been sold. In the same way, you need to determine what makes your product special. What makes your company brand special? It is part of your work as a salesperson to know this, because that's where your source of confidence comes from, and that's what the market will receive and buy.

The other special way to develop that confidence is through building credibility through the successes of your past. Great salespeople can tell stories about how their solutions made a difference in other people's lives. Let's take the example of a person looking for a job. The employee that will talk about their past achievements in their previous jobs and can back that up with verifiable evidence is likely to get the job than a person who has no track record. People always want to know if your services have been used elsewhere and what difference they made.

As a great salesperson, you must recognise the times where you have made a difference. Then you need to know how to be a great storyteller that describes how your intervention made that difference. If you have several stories like that, you have a great collection of those in your head, and you tell the stories well when the selling moments come your way, then you are becoming the great salesperson that you need to become. Learn to see the difference that you are making. Learn to see the difference that your product or service is making. Learn to see the difference that your company is making in the marketplace. Once you equip yourself with that knowledge and you craft the stories of how you made that difference, your confidence shoots up, and the market will reward you greatly for your confidence.

Ask For Assistance

Entrepreneurial people are usually independent in their thinking and may not want the feeling of being controlled or to be told what to do. However, most of the entrepreneurs I have seen, talked to, and researched about have such an unquenchable desire to learn such that they look for professional help to get their stuff together.

There is humility in them that allows them to know when they need to attend conferences, appoint board members to their companies, and look for mentorship from people who have travelled on this journey before. The interesting thing about these people is that they don't just look for professional advice on their ventures, they also look for professional help in their personal lives. They are so in touch with themselves as they are with their organisations.

As individuals who are hunting for treasures inside of us, we need to realise that sometimes it takes other people to identify and point out this treasure in us. It may also take other people to assist us in seeing the stumbling blocks that are hindering us from getting to our wealth.

Let's start with looking for personal assistance for personal challenges. Over the years, I have had to unlearn some things that I had taken for granted, which then affected me negatively. I was trapped into a negative habit that began to get a serious hold on my life. It became more powerful than a habit and started bordering on the lines of addiction. Being a church guy in a leadership position, I convinced myself that I would sort this out on my own and with my God without involving other people. However, beneath that was a particular pride that stopped me from opening up to my elders or pastors about my challenges. There was fear of being judged after appearing to be super strong all the time. I also did not consider looking for other professional counselling or help to sort this out. That was the last thing on my mind. It was not part of my problem-solving culture. I had not experienced it in my upbringing and did not consider it necessary.

It was only when the habit began to destroy the things I cared about that I started looking for help. It took some critical people in my life to walk away, some personal financial losses and deep emotional pain for me to start looking for assistance. I reached a stage where I had to find help from people I didn't know and had never met. I ended up looking for professional therapists and joining help groups for assistance. At that time, looking for spiritual support in the church was no longer just an option to consider.

I searched for help with so much urgency, and surprisingly, I found that assistance. It took some time going through this counselling and assistance, and slowly, I began to come back to my senses. It even cost me money that I didn't have at the time. What I uncovered there was something that opened up a world of discoveries about myself that helped me understand cause and effect.

I learnt that the negative habit that I had taken up as a result of me trying to musk the emotional pain that I could not deal with. Many men suffer from this. They are told that they should always look and act strong such that they cannot get in touch with their emotions. The black African men like me are the worst hit. This is why we sometimes don't acknowledge illnesses like depression which can lead to mental illness or even lead people to commit suicide. Some musk their pain in drugs and alcohol. On the outside, it looks like you are searching for fun and pleasure, but in reality, you are running away from the internal pain and turmoil that you cannot deal with.

I also learnt that part of the pain I was experiencing was coming from my childhood experiences. The great thing is that I could unpack those experiences with the help of the professionals. The experiences looked minor to me, and I thought they had no effect or hold on me. The truth is that they still had a stronghold in my life. They were now showing up in my professional and personal life. This was also a tough thing for me to acknowledge. In our culture, our "upbringing" and "childhood pain" are not subjects that one can easily talk about. The values of respect we are taught sometimes go beyond respect and border on the lines of fear of confronting the truth. Here I was, trying to uncover this as an adult, and having to deal with these issues.

As I began to recover from this depression and the unhealthy habits, I started thinking about how many other young men like me were going through the same stuff, had gone through the same pain and were holding back from looking for help. I am now more in touch with myself because of that painful experience. It has taught me to look for help whenever I have a problem. It has taught me even to consult professionals.

Let me address some men and women who may be suffering from that depression right now, and are trying hard to hide it and even suppress it through some unhealthy habits. I want to say to you; it's okay to be in that space. You are not alone. I also want to tell you that it's okay to look for professional assistance and counselling. It's not a weakness at all. We are all human, and we have our challenges. Some people have studied and been trained to help you uncover the issues and assist you with navigating through that journey. Make use of them. Call for help. Don't be embarrassed to do this, and don't wait for things to go bad before you start looking for assistance. Your emotional pain is an indicator that you need some healing, and you need to allow for that process to take place.

The last lesson I leant from that experience is that you may be religious but not submit to the power and assistance of God. I was doing everything in the religious circles, but I was missing the point of surrendering my issues to my Creator. The biggest reason for my failure to submit to God's help and assistance was that I had a distorted view of who He is. I pictured a strict father who was waiting to expose my every wrong and punish me for everything I was doing wrong. That mental distortion blocked me from fully surrendering to God's unconditional love, power, and grace. Once I had a glimpse of His unending grace and love, change began to happen from the inside out, and I learnt to trust in Him with all I have. I am still learning to do so, and maybe you can join me on that journey, too. So yes, let's learn to ask for help.

The Three Fundamentals of a Great Vision

For us to multiply our efforts, we must see beyond what others see. That is important. If we combine that powerful vision with the ability to communicate that vision in such a way that it influences people to follow our dream, then already, our efforts will have the potential to multiply. When those efforts are multiplied, our value is multiplied as well, as we now have many heads, hearts, and minds working on the vision we carry.

So, let us talk about the key ways to make sure that your vision is powerful and persuasive. There are three essential aspects of a vision. Combined, these three pillars enable us to fully persuade people. If one is missing, then our ability to persuade is reduced significantly.

These three pillars are found in Aristotle's '**The Rhetoric**', and they are:

1. Logos or Logic
2. Pathos or Passion
3. Ethos of Ethics

A good vision must be logical. It must make sense to those who follow it. This means it must appeal to the minds of the followers. When the vision is not specific, measurable, achievable, result-oriented, and time-bound, people will see its weaknesses and choose not to follow the vision and the vision bearer. The followers must be able to follow the reason why this vision is essential to them. The more benefits and the positive impact it will have on them and society, the more it's pulling power. A good leader must, therefore, be able to show the logic and action steps they will take to make sure that the vision is achieved. If the action steps shown do not make sense to the followers, the ability to multiply the visionary's efforts are taken down.

The second pillar of a powerful vision is passion. In other words, the vision should appeal not only to the minds (logic) but also to the hearts of the people. I have a passion for real estate investment, so I usually follow property developers when they promote a residential property that they are about to develop. Most houses are generally sold way before the structures are erected on the ground, and this is partly because the developers know how to appeal to the hearts of home buyers. Instead of showing the strength of the building material used in the building, they will show pictures of happy families around the complex. It could be couples going for a jog around the beautiful complex, or kids playing in the swimming pool. They are appealing to the hearts of potential buyers. The buyers are not just buying an empty building; they are buying family bliss. In the same way, your vision must appeal to the hearts.

On the same aspect of passion, the visionary must show that they have enough passion for following through the vision to the end. If the followers do not see how passionate we are, they are not likely to put their lives on the line, because it shows that we do not believe in what we are doing. Former US President Barack Obama's "Yes We Can" slogan caught the hearts of many US voters and many around the world. He said it with the passion that captured the hearts of many in his 2008 campaign. As you can see, passion reduced to simplified statements can allow many to buy in and follow your vision.

The last pillar of a vision is the ethics behind the visionaries. This speaks to the character of the visionary. People need to trust the visionary for them to buy into the vision and become promoters of the vision. This talks to issues of integrity, honesty, and accountability. The higher we climb the corporate ladder, the more visible we are to those who follow us. They follow every word and action we say, do, and can read even the smallest of details. Any sign of a crack in the ethics will make them run away.

Do we do what we say? Who are we when no one is looking? Do we take responsibility for our mistakes when we make mistakes? There are many stories of great leaders who when the weaknesses in their characters were revealed; everyone around them started running away. Sponsors stopped funding their initiatives, staff members began resigning, voters looked for other alternatives, and some close family members chose to step away from them. This pillar is, therefore, essential for any visionary.

We are generally attracted to men and women of good character. That does not mean we should become perfect people, as that is impossible, but we must strive to be the best that we can be. When we make mistakes, we must own up to them and try to fix whatever wrong we have done. Character is usually a result of the company we keep, the messages we hear, and the choices we make. The topic of leadership will show more of how we can build our characters and become visionaries that have an impact in this world.

The Habit Of Identifying Opportunities And Taking Advantage Of Them

In addition to the habit of problem-solving, people with an entrepreneurial mindset can see when opportunities are knocking at their doors. They can see beyond the small door that has been opened, to imagine what other doors could be opened and how they can have them opened.

Let's define what an opportunity is, first, so that we know what we are talking about. I want to define an opportunity as a rare moment/occurrence which if seized, will lead to remarkable progress in an area of your life or the life of your organisation. I say rare because moments/occurrences are not easily identifiable, nor do they come every day in the same way. It is also essential to specify that they are momentary because opportunities are usually short-lived. This is where the great man called Leonard Ravenhill said: "an opportunity of a lifetime must be seized in the lifetime of the opportunity".

Now that we know what an opportunity is, let's talk about examples of people that identified opportunities and seized them in their lifetime, leading to significant progress in their lives.

I am reminded of an opportunity that took place in Silulo Ulutho Technologies, where I used to work. My former boss, the Founder of Silulo, Mr Luvuyo Rani, had been nominated for an award for his outstanding contribution in the Social entrepreneurship sphere. The program was called the Ten Outstanding Young Persons of the world. Although he knew about the nomination, he had not gotten enough information to see how this award nomination could open bigger doors of progress for the company.

The opportunity came closer when the results of the nomination were announced. He had been shortlisted among the twenty outstanding leaders for the year 2014. He quickly went to the website to see what the other nineteen nominees had achieved in their different spheres, and who had received the same award in the past. For him to be in the final list of ten, he had to get votes from the public within two weeks.

I remember seeing him come to my office saying, "Unos, I had not seen that this award could be a game-changer for us, but after having gone through the website, I now see clearly that we have to seize this opportunity that the man above has given."

I could see that the tone had changed, priorities shifted, and suddenly, this rare moment was being given prime attention by the highest-ranking officer in our organisation. In the next few days, he formulated a strategy, held a meeting with his fellow directors and management team, and together came up with ideas of how to get the needed votes.

Using his already-high social media presence and the organisation's retail outlets, all customers and supporters of his business got to know about this nomination, and then the votes started coming. One person in the organisation was tasked to keep track of how the votes were going and if we were doing well there. As if that was not enough, Luvuyo used that very nomination to take the company profile forward into the local and national media houses. He knew that it was the prime time of the opportunity, and thus it gave the audience rare information that in turn grew the brand of his organisation. When the two weeks came to an end, our organisation was up there, having received publicity worth millions at no cost to us.

When he finally got the news that he was part of the ten outstanding young persons of the world, he did not just sit and celebrate. He realised that another opportunity had been opened for more stakeholders to know about our high impact organisation. Emails went out to partners, customers, funders, and potential collaborators. Throughout the time of that rare opportunity, I remember seeing how more nominations for the organisation started coming and how potential funders were knocking on our doors to see how they could partner with this growing social media enterprise.

There are several lessons about opportunities that can be taken from this story.

1. When an opportunity knocks on your door, it is seemingly small. It does not shout. It seeks your

attention and response as in the case of how he got nominated.

2. As you get to the middle of this rare moment in time, opportunity starts shouting and becomes more visible to you. At that moment, you have to leave all else and pursue her. She will not stop for you, but you have to stop for her, organise your team and run for her in the time she has demanded.

Opportunity is the boss here, not the one who needs it. If you do not give her priority, she keeps walking away and soon enough, you will see her no more. What opportunities are open in your life today? If you are a student at school and exams are about to come, this is a time to give your studies a big chunk of your time. As you focus on the exam, you get to understand that rare moment very well and master the subject, preparing yourself for that three-hour moment where you have to demonstrate your knowledge. As an entrepreneur, you need to take time to understand what's happening in your business and what you are planning.

When that moment comes when your potential investor gives you three minutes to sell your story, you should hit all the essential aspects of your business that your investor wants to know about. If you are in a music group, there is a rare moment that will come, where a universally renowned recording and marketing brand will watch your performance. When that moment comes, your team should be prepared to give their all into that song. I guess you get the point now. Preparation is the word that sums it all up. Miracles happen when opportunity meets preparation. How much time are you taking to prepare yourself for that moment?

3. At the end of the opportunity cycle, the opportunity will tempt you to relax and celebrate. That's the time you should be asking her the question, "What other doors can you open for me?" You may have noticed that I started describing opportunity as a thing and ended up referring to opportunity as a person? That's because I realised that opportunity has a life and follows a specific pattern that's similar to how humans behave.

Back to more doors opening. Let me give a few examples. There is a story in the Bible about a young man called Joseph. Joseph had a dream of something big that was going to happen in the future. Unfortunately, his brothers were jealous of this dream, and that's where opportunity started building up for Joseph. How did that happen? The brothers beat him up, threw him in a pit and sold him to strangers as a slave. Being the problem-solver that he was, Joseph excelled at his assignment as a slave and found favour with his boss. Two more problems came into his life that led him to prison. He was wrongfully accused of having attempted to accost his boss's wife and ended up in jail. Being the problem-solver that he was, again, Joseph kept helping others, including two fellow prisoners who needed to solve the problem of interpretation of dreams. Capitalising on his relationship with the God to whom his father had introduced him, he managed to break the code and gave them exact interpretations of their dreams.

The last opportunity that needed his attention was a dream from the king, which many had failed to interpret. Due to being the well-known problem solver, one of his former beneficiaries or clients gave him a resounding referral and told the king that there was a prisoner who specialised in solving these kinds of problems. When he was called, he made use of that evident and loud opportunity to interpret the dream of the king. At the climax of this opportunity, he had been appointed governor in a foreign land, but he was wise enough to ask for more.

When he saw that a famine had troubled his brothers and parents, he asked for permission to have them migrate and live with him so that they would have enough supplies. He ended up saving his whole generation by solving problems and seizing opportunities as they presented themselves. Can you see how his value multiplied? From being a slave to becoming a governor; second in command to the king. From working for nothing to becoming a millionaire and a philanthropist. This ancient story is packed with lessons we can apply in our daily lives and the marketplace.

To conclude, I would say that opportunities usually come disguised as problems. Only the person who is used to solving problems will turn them into profitable opportunities. Once the opportunities become clear, they often show up in tiny ways, which is the time where we need to give them our attention. At the end of that opportunity, we should be asking for more before they die and manifest in another different way.

The Habit Of Disciplined Focus

The problems we face in society have different levels of complexity/seriousness. So, as much as our value increases when we solve problems, it also depends on how serious or complex those problems are. Ordinary, common problems have a low-value tag. As they become more sophisticated, problems also call for a better problem-solver. As the problems become more complicated, you find that the people who can provide solutions to those problems become fewer. These few problem-solvers now have a right to charge higher prices for their time and effort, because they are not dealing with ordinary problems.

I saw this when I went through training at PWC as an articled clerk. As a first-year clerk, I would spend many hours at a client working on a specific section of the audit, which was considered comfortable and straightforward by the rest of the team. Trainee auditors knew that they would work on sections like Cash and Bank, or Property Plant and Equipment. I figured that when we charged the client, we were using the number of hours that the team spent working at the client. As the most junior clerk, I would have the most hours worked, but my rate was the lowest.

For example, where the client was charged 50 dollars per hour for my work as a first-year clerk, they would be charged 500 dollars an hour for the time that the partner (highest-ranking officer on the job) spent. This was because of the difference in the problem-solving ability that we had as well as the complexity of the problems we had to face. Not much expertise was needed for someone to perform audit procedures on Bank and Cash, but so much more was demanded from the partner. He was accountable for the whole audit and ensuring that the financial information presented by the client was free from material mis-statements. His signature as the partner was so essential and so the value of one hour was ten times more than that of a junior clerk with little experience or qualification.

The same applies to the medical profession. There are problems that nurses can deal with on their own, but they reach a ceiling in their level of problem-solving. They then refer the problem to the medical doctor, who is usually a general practitioner. The general practitioner also has a ceiling in terms of the level of complexity that he can deal with, and so he ends up referring the problem to a specialist doctor. Due to the difference in the level of problems that these individuals can deal with, they get paid at different rates.

I'm sure that by now you can see that for your value to increase, you need to solve complex problems in your field. Even in business, the companies that can solve more complex problems in their field also get to name their price more. They would have perfected their work such that they can charge a higher price.

This level of specialty does not just happen. It comes through years of individual or institutional experience that gives individual or institutional value. This is why you need to choose your area of focus and begin to go deeper into that area. As you specialise as a company or as an individual, perfect your problem-solving skillset and then charge more for your time. However, if you are a jack of all trades, you specialise in solving low-value problems, thus you earn low value in money. The more comprehensive your skillset is; the more people can replace you. In business, there is what they call "barriers of entry". There are industries where only those with certain levels of experience and qualifications can qualify to operate. Focus and disciplined use of time, therefore, becomes important.

How do we reach this level of discipline and focus? We reach this level of discipline and focus when we know who we are, where we are going, and what we want to focus on. Focus or discipline is a product of vision. This is why great men and women are called visionaries. They identify where they want to go and articulate that vision so well that everyone begins to focus their energies on that destination. The vision, therefore, tells the team what to focus on and what to leave as they work. Vision provides direction and removes all distractions along the way. A person working towards becoming a medical doctor focuses on identifying a medical school and therefore will not find himself even considering applying to a law school.

Although law school would be a great option, it will not be in the vision, and therefore it becomes a distraction.

Vision motivates us in the times when we are tired. We keep seeing the place we are supposed to go and how reaching that goal will make us feel. That pulls us to working harder for the promise that lies ahead.

The Habit Of Gaining The Cooperation Of Others To Achieve Desired Results

In the first part of this book, I talked about how you could maximise your value through personal development. This included understanding that you are a person of serious value, understanding that you have a unique SHAPE, and investing in the four Es of developing the treasure in you (Education, Exposure, Experience and Execution). These principles maximise your internal value. In other words, where you could earn 200 dollars as you invest in this, you start seeing your value multiply to 2000 or going to 20 000 dollars in how much you can earn at a job or in your line of work.

Tremendous value starts coming up, and job hunters start looking for your unique expertise. Suddenly, countries want to allow you to become a permanent resident in their nation. You are now among the rare few, and therefore funds start fighting for your attention.

However, your value would have been multiplied in part. There is another factor now, that if used well, could add more zeros to your value. What this factor does is that it takes your current value, and it replicates the things you can achieve. You begin to have more heads thinking about your vision, more hands working on your purpose, and more hearts pushing for your cause. That factor is called the influence factor. Yes, you've got it. The element is called leadership.

Many books have been written about leadership, and I suggest that you begin to invest in reading them. I want to ignite your passion for developing your leadership capabilities and give you the over-arching principles that guide your leadership development. Once you have started taking leadership development more seriously, I do not doubt that your value will multiply in ways that even you cannot explain.

So, here are a few principles you should take note of in your leadership journey.

1. Every human being has serious value. They deserve to be treated with dignity and honour. Just in the same

way we talked about you understanding that you have serious value, you need to understand that all people around you also have the value that needs to be respected, recognised, and honoured.

No effective leader will treat people like lesser human beings. If they have a position of influence, they have to fight to keep it, and they will soon lose that position. The human spirit always rises above the discrimination of one against the other, because we were all created to have dominion over all the earth and live harmoniously in a way that can benefit all of us. Concepts such as slavery, colonialism, imperialism, and apartheid could not survive the test of time. In the same way, concepts that see a different gender as less valuable will not stand the test of time. Once you begin to understand this, you are shaping your leadership philosophy.

2. Treating people with dignity is the first step toward influence. Intuitively, all human beings know that they have value. When you show that you recognise that value, they gravitate towards you because you are bringing out who they truly are inside. What you are doing is giving them a gift of honour, which they may not have received as they grew up because they were raised in a place where people around them had not grasped this critical concept.

   Sometimes, you are giving them a gift that they have not learnt to give to themselves. You are helping them see value in themselves and to stop self-hate, self-sabotage, and self-pity. You are removing them from self-made prisons and chains. You are becoming a liberator. You are becoming a leader.

   There is a story in the Bible about David running away from Saul, the king who felt threatened by the young David and was determined to kill him. David ran to a cave called the cave of Adullam. He was distressed and fearful when his family and a bunch of 400 distressed folks came to be with him in that cave. Here is how the Bible describes this team of people. *"And everyone who was in distress, everyone who was in debt, and everyone who was discontented gathered to him. So he became captain over them. And there were about four hundred men with him."* **1 Samuel 22:2.**

There are two lessons that you can derive.

> a. What drew many people to David were his previous accomplishments, mainly that he had managed to kill Goliath, a man whom many feared. He had perfected his skills of war and used them at the right time and suddenly stood out from the rest. That was the first part of multiplying his value.

> b. When his family and the four hundred distressed men came to him, he started taking care of them and sought a place of refuge for them in Moab, far from King Saul. In other words, he recognised the value in them and sought to protect the seemingly valueless human beings. That is how David increased his influence. As you continue reading his story, you will find out that these distressed men later became courageous battle warriors who fought alongside David and defended his honour. All this happened because David respected them and acknowledged their dignity and right to life at a time when their king wanted them destroyed and dead. David became a man of significance and influence because he treated people with respect.

3. A good leader identifies talents and abilities and delegates tasks accordingly.

    Leaders are great at spotting talent. They can pick it up from the darkest of places because they have developed the eye that can see potential and what that potential can be turned into. They see the raw talent, and they know that they can nurture and train that talent to become better than it is.

    One of my favourite gospel groups is Joyous Celebration, and I have followed their story for years now. I'm a serious fan. I would buy a ticket and fly to a different city to attend their show. The group has produced some of the best gospel musicians in South Africa. When you listen to the story of how some of them were recruited into the team, you see how serious they are about identifying talent. Some went through a rigorous audition in their city. Some were spotted at funerals while they were busy mourning their beloved in song. Some were picked out from church while they were leading worship and unaware that their recruiters were watching. The directors have developed an eye for the specific talent that fits into their purpose, and when they see it, they take it.

    What kind of talent do you need in your organisation or business? Can you spot that talent? Has your ear been trained to be like Director Lindelani — who can pick a potential lead singer at a funeral? If not, start training yourself to do that.

    4. Great leaders equip their teams with the right tools, so that they multiply their value.

    Do you remember those four Es (Education, Experience, Exposure, and Execution) of personal development? Great leaders not only invest in their development by working on their four Es, but they equip their teams with the relevant four Es, so that they can achieve the best. I saw a quote from Sir Richard Branson that said something like this: "Train your employees so well that they can leave, treat them so well so that they want to stay." I thought that was profound. It is a combination of equipping and respecting people so that they still want to work with you. Great leaders are not threatened by developing their teams. They are secure in who they are. They love it when they can be replaced because they can then focus on higher goals. They train others to take their place so that they have time to create higher places as they multiply their vision because they are continuously learning and developing. Oh, my God! That's deep, right? Oh yeah! I just shouted Amen in my room. Hahaha! That leads me to the next principle of leadership.

5. Great leaders are visionaries. Remember that when we talked about developing yourself, we referred to your ambitions and tapped into your vision. That was intentional, because that is an essential aspect of leadership. Leaders see further than those who follow them. Indeed, they can see what's present and close, but they have also trained their eyes to see beyond the visible. They have made use of that tool that is more powerful than education. The tool of imagination. They take time to think about where they want to go and where they want their organisation to go. If you want to develop your vision, please revisit the chapter on **Understanding your SHAPE**, especially on the Heart. I dealt with the issue of ambition and gave some tasks that can guide you into how to start mapping your vision. If you are setting a vision for the organisation and you want to build a vision together, you can do that I many ways, but I have found these four questions easy and straightforward to follow.

   a. If you were to read about your organisation in the next five to ten years, what would you like the headlines to be? Describe briefly what that newspaper article would say about the organisation's accomplishments.

b. What things should you stop doing for you to reach that vision?

c. What things should you continue doing to reach that vision?

d. What new things should you start doing to get to that vision?

When you and your team start answering these questions, you are stretching your imagination and creating something tangible from the invisible and intangible things. You are exercising your God-given dominion, and it does not only feel good, but it is also absolutely fantastic. Your vision begins to guide and take you to places you've never been.

6. Great leaders are great communicators. Not only do they see the future, but they can communicate that future so well that it becomes clear to those that listen. The communication of their vision ignites the imaginative capabilities of their stakeholders and suddenly creates the excitement that makes funders run to them with their money, employees run to them with their skills, sponsors want to associate with that vision, and customers want to consume their products. Like every skill, the skill of communication can be developed. It is an art that can be developed through training and practice. I have seen people who were timid and shy turning into great orators. I have seen people who could not write anything convincing turn into authors and great persuaders. We can all learn this art. Some places specialise in teaching these skills. Places like Toastmasters. Join such organisations and follow their programs.

Some places can train you to exercise all these leadership principles and get to multiply your value. One such place in which I have invested my time in is called JCI (Junior Chamber International). I find that whenever I take on a project at JCI, and I become part of the team. I always learn something new about leadership. I learn through practice. You can read all you want, but you also need a place where you can exercise these principles. You can even do it at your local church or social club. Better still, exercise these principles in your workplace and your business. The more time you get to exercise your leadership muscle, the more value you get and the more valuable you become. The more valuable you become, the more happiness, health, and wealth you attract.

The Habit Of Identifying Problems And Creating Solutions

Every big business that you know is providing a solution to some problem faced in the community. Those who face the effects of that problem automatically become the potential customer base of that business. Solving problems is the essence of all entrepreneurial endeavours known to man. The grocery stores in your neighbourhood identified the distance problem that you and others in your community were facing as you had to travel to the closest shopping mall, which meant that you had to drive or get a taxi to get there before you could buy a loaf of bread. To solve the problem, they brought the store closer to you. Beyond that, they are providing convenience to you. Instead of you having to go to the huge bakeries that are in the business of baking bread, they decided to acquire the bread for you, to separate it from the huge bread boxes that bakeries put the bread into, and placed the loaf of bread on a shelf that's visible to you so you can easily reach it.

The same goes for all social enterprises. Think about a church/mosque, for example. What problem is that organisation solving? Well, it answers the deep invisible spiritual void that all human beings have, that which seeks the guidance and love of the Higher Power. The church, therefore, provides a service where you can meet with other believers and hear what the Higher Power is saying to the people. The liquor store is solving a problem of thirst, boredom, loneliness, and sometimes depression. Although that solution may be temporary, the customers know that they are getting something to relieve their pain.

What I have described above is the simplest way of understanding how value is created. The better you get at providing solutions to the society's problems, the more valuable you become as a person. If you can scale up and solve as many issues as possible in any given time, the wealthier you become in whatever way you perceive wealth. In the same way, the highest-paid employee in any company is the one who can provide the best solutions for the organisation. It could be through giving out his knowledge to other team members so that they are sure of what they are doing, or it could be through the gift of inspiring others to produce more out of what they have. Whatever it is, that general relationship governs how value is created in the world.

So, two habits are part of problem-solving. One is the ability to identify the problem, and the other one is the ability to solve the problem. The first one sounds so simple, but it may not be as simple as it sounds. Whatever problem that society encounters cannot be solved until society identifies and names the cause of the problem. Those who take time to analyse and verbalise the problem usually starts identifying what the problem is. Sometimes what is verbalised are the results of the problem and not the actual problem. An inquisitive mind is what is needed for us to identify problems. This is why all successful companies conduct market research. As an individual, the inquisitive mind should always lead you to ask questions and find answers from the people you wish to serve.

In his book, Mr Raymond Ackerman passes on a personal problem-solving formula that he learnt from his professor, and he still uses now. The solution involves writing down answers to six simple questions. There is something that begins to happen when we start writing and describing where we are. I have often used this same method in my challenges, and I find it useful. It makes things clear. If you master this art in your tailored way, I assure you that you are already different from many people that are used to crying and whining about their problems and not solving them.

It's not enough to be an employee who does the expected. What will you do if unexpected challenges come into your department? If you are the go-to person for problem-solving, soon enough, your pay should go up. If you are prepared adequately, you can foresee challenges and prepare for them in such a way that the people in your organisation know that you are the rare breed. The more you become rare and special, the more value you get.

For organisational challenges, I find this formula by a non-profit company called the 3 Day Start-Up quite easy to follow. They took their time to study what successful entrepreneurs do to meet the needs of their markets and become profitable in the shortest time. Over time, they came up with a simple description that could also help you improve your entrepreneurial endeavours in your organisation or a new venture. I have put brief explanations to each of the questions that they came up with so that they offer guidance. Once again, I recommend that you write so that your mind becomes clear about what the problem is and what the possible solutions could be.

As you repeat this habit, you may find that you now become an intuitive problem-solver and no longer need to take some of the steps word for word. Some steps you will do faster, just like one learns how to drive. The first time you drive a manual car, everything is a challenge, but as you get used to it, you start changing gears, pressing the clutch and accelerator in a coordinated natural way that you don't even realise that you are doing it.

So, let's get to it. Like any habit, it takes time to master. Keep coming back to this chapter when you face any problem and see if these steps will not give you a better outcome than when you constantly worry about what's happening to you.

The Problem-Solving Process

1. Define the problem. The best way to do this is to write it down in as much detail as possible — describing what the issue is and how it is affecting you or your organisation.
2. Determine the root cause(s) of the problem. List down the root causes as they come into your mind. Put as much detail to each cause as you see necessary.
3. Develop alternative solutions. In this stage, you start writing down all the possible solutions. As you were writing the root causes, some possible solutions were coming into your mind already.
4. Rank the solutions and select a solution on which you want to work.
5. Develop an action plan for the solution you have chosen, and start working on it.
6. Evaluate the outcome.

The 5 Minute Pitch Process by the 3 Day Start Up

The ideal 5 minute pitch to investors:

1. Defines the PROBLEM
2. Gives the idea of the MARKET SIZE
3. Describes the SOLUTION
4. Has a clear REVENUE MODEL
5. Shows the COMPETETIVE LANDSCAPING
6. Has a GO TO MARKET STRATEGY
7. Shows the TEAM behind the idea

The Power Of An Engaged Citizen

THERE IS INEXPLICABLE joy and happiness that fills our hearts when we start living a life of service to others. We were wired not only to dominate the earth and subdue it, but to serve one another. We were wired to need one another for us to live a happy and fulfilled life. What does this have to do with multiplying your value? It has everything to do with your value. Your value is not measured only in monetary terms or in the wealth you have. What good is money when you are sick and unhappy? No, we must aim to be wealthy, healthy, and happy people. It is my observation that if we want to live a happy life, we will find that happiness as we serve others and meet their needs. The re-energizing feeling we get in serving others pulls us through so many nightmares and times of despair.

What is service? It is the action of helping or doing work for someone. It is synonymous to giving an act of assistance, good turn, favour, kindness, helping hand, or aid. For someone to develop a culture of service, there must be a reason why they do it, and it must come from a deep-seated set of beliefs that inspires them to serve.

Africa needs this culture of service greatly. Africa consistently displays this culture of service, often called Ubuntu, where we value the other person because we see ourselves in them. That is why in our upbringing, a child is raised by a community and not just by biological parents. Sadly, this culture has not sunk deep into the institutions that we have built or that have been handed to us after the colonial era. It may be deep sitting in the family setup, but it indeed has not yielded the benefits to many of the African countries.

I firmly believe that this is because the educational system that introduces all of us to the field of work has not emphasised the importance of this value. Therefore, we destroy one another and take advantage of one another through the rampant corruption that is stopping our progress. Learning mathematics is as important as receiving a values-based education. It is as essential as teaching servant leadership if not more important. We cannot have leaders that are technically competent and yet impoverished in the values that make us who we are.

Allow me to define the origin of service in my way. Service, as shown in the definition above, is a verb, an action that benefits the other person. In other words, it is a result of a thought process that comes from a set of values. If we were to look at it in terms of vegetation, service would be the fruit, the thoughts that produce the service would be the trunk, and the values would be the roots of the tree. For us to produce the fruit of service, we must get the roots right. They must be in the right environment, and they must be fed with the correct nutrients for us to think right and produce right. Here is a set of values that I believe produce the culture of service.

1. **Respect for human dignity.** Before we serve others, we must first believe that human beings are sacred. Before we believe that others are sacred, we must believe that we are sacred. Dr Martin Luther King put it this way in one of his speeches to a group of learners.

"Number one in your life's blueprint should be a deep belief in your dignity, your worth, and your somebody-ness. Don't allow anybody to make you feel that you are nobody. Always

feel that you count. Always feel that you have worth, and always feel that your life has ultimate significance."

Any person who believes strongly in their "somebody-ness" has started on a good foundation in terms of respecting human dignity. We can only respect others if we have given ourselves the honour of self-respect. It is easier for us to see others in the same way when we believe that we are important. However, if we have grown up with the belief that our opinion does not matter, that our voice does not count, we may likely violate the right of others to voice out their opinions and for us to give them the respect they deserve.

As I write this part of the book, I have been watching two stories develop in my country of birth Zimbabwe, and my current country of residence, South Africa. In Zimbabwe, the government has responded to the public protests over price hikes by unleashing the army into the people's houses and city streets. Many are being beaten, so many have been imprisoned, some have been killed, and some have serious injuries due to this intervention. I firmly believe that this is a fruit of self-hate from the leadership of our country. If they had just a little bit of self-respect and respect for human dignity, they would have reacted differently. The culture of abuse and disrespect for human rights is one that has been so entrenched in our society that the leaders choose to silence their people instead of listening to their legitimate cries over the economic suffering the nation is going through. Nevertheless, again, when you look at the background of the leaders in charge, you understand that the roots have not yet been dealt with properly.

How can they produce a different fruit from what they have known for the more significant part of their lives? They faced a ruthless colonial government, and when it was their time to lead, they adopted some of the tactics of their former enemies because that was what was deeply rooted in them. People were not meant to be listened to. Civilians were supposed to just obey and follow whatever the government declared, and so, although they desire to lead a democratic government, the seed or root of democracy was never in them. They will need to work hard on their mindset for them to start reacting differently. Otherwise, they will resort to their normal wiring.

Here in South Africa, the revelations of the Zondo Commission on State Capture show the mindset of the Zuma administration. It is a scarcity mindset, one that says: "It's our time now. We had better eat now, or we will forever starve." In this mindset, you only look after yourself and your family as you maximise the opportunity to loot. There can never be enough for everyone, therefore, those in power should take advantage of the time they have been given.

It is a dangerous mindset because it assumes that everyone should also be thinking that way. Everyone has a price. They can all be bought. Some private sector companies saw this, and they started giving monthly bribes to high-ranking officials in whom the public had vested their trust. That way of thinking also comes from the experience of oppression and exclusion. The African leader has to consciously work on his way of thinking, seek other sources of value, and constantly renew his mind for him to move away from this scarcity and dictatorial mindset.

It has to be replaced with the mindset that believes that everyone is important. Their voices and outcries are worth the listen. The corruption mindset also has to be replaced with the value that acknowledges that the public trusted me with their votes because they wanted me to do my best for them, not just for myself.

2. **The values of Accountability & Transparency.** This is vital for all meaningful relationships we have in life. From spousal, parental, business, national to international relations, people rise and fall because of the availability or lack of these values.

At a national level or global level, financial institutions want to work with countries that have transparent and accountable leadership, so that they manage their risks. They want to know if they will get their money back and if the policy environment will not just change any day to their disadvantage. There is also an interesting relationship between the level of economic development of countries and their ability to be transparent and accountable. To see this, have a look at this 2018 report from Transparency International online www.transparency.org/ cpi2018.

I certainly agree that some of this is about perceptions, which stresses the point further. The more corrupt a county is perceived to be; the less investment it will attract generally. At a business level, investors also want to know if the companies they are dealing with have the right values and principles that will allow them to monitor the performance of their stock. Employees want to know if the company treats employees with the dignity and respect that they deserve, and they will enquire from other people before they apply. Customers want to buy products and services from companies that they can trust. Take the Steinhoff or KPMG incidents. When the market received the news that the leadership of the company was cooking the books to make the company look better, the stock lost its value.

At a personal level, your value can fall instantly when you fail to follow this principle as well. Many divorce cases also come about because of a lack of accountability and transparency. When a spouse finds out that her partner has been hiding some money and sending it to his parents without her knowledge, the drama starts.

It is therefore important that we make this value a part of our normal lifestyle. There is no point in working so hard to build our value and then see it crash in an instant when the truth about our dealings surface. We should build from a good foundation — where there is nothing to hide. Admittedly, this is better said than done, and we are not perfect, but if we are serious about multiplying our value, then, by all means, we have to value transparency and accountability.

3. **Civic Education.** Civic education teaches us about how our countries' political systems work. We learn what our rights and duties are as citizens and how to take part in the decision-making process.

As much as it is essential to learn about history, literature and mathematics in school, it is equally important to equip our citizens with the knowledge of how communities work, about the relationship between government, business, civil society, and about what role we can play to make our community better. This type of education could be improved in Africa. History teaches us about what happens in the past, but civic education empowers us to build the future that we want as society.

In the absence of great formal civic education, the African citizen must learn how to find this wealth of knowledge and use it to their advantage. As Africans, we cannot afford not to be interested in how our politics works and how the resources of our continent are used. We can only do that at our peril. Politics may not be our calling, passion or inclination, but unfortunately, it does affect us directly and indirectly. We must learn about how better-performing countries are governed, how the citizens engage, and how they make it work for them. We also have to come up with the solutions that make our environment better for us and all who are around us.

As I am on this subject, let me give you a few statistics we should note.

- Over 625 million people are without power in Sub-Saharan Africa alone – that's 68% of the population.
- In Northern Africa, one in four youth is living in abject poverty. While twelve million youth enter the job market each year across the continent, only three secure formal jobs.
- Over 50% of the world's extreme poor, or individuals living on less than $1.90 a day live in Africa, the majority of whom are under fifteen years of age. While Africa is only home to 16% of the world's population, they are home to 50% of the world's impoverished.
- Each year, 25% of the continent's GDP or $148 billion is drained out of the continent away from its citizens because of corruption. In 2017 alone, 75 million

Africans claimed they had paid a bribe within the last year.

- According to Transparency International, only six out of the fifty-four African states scored above fifty on the transparency index.

Although most countries of the world (2/3) are below this score, one would have expected that we at least, have one third 1/3 (18 countries) as a starting point, but that is not the case. What this means is that the poorest of the poor in our countries will fail to have access to free health care, because a few people are taking advantage of their access to power and pubic resources, which they will use for their gain. It also means that the normal services that we are supposed to receive for our roads, schools, and water systems are compromised.

We thank our forefathers and foremothers for the work they did as they fought to liberate Africa from colonial rule. It was a ruthless form of oppression and one that could be easily identified. It is now our season to fight our battles for our sake and future generations. The enemy of this day is no longer as clearly identifiable as colonial rule was in yester-years. It is no longer just drawn along racial lines. It is subtler and yet way more dangerous for our generation and our future. Almost all African countries conduct elections and profess to live by principles of democracy, the rule of law and constitutionalism, but in practice, that is hardly the case. The vast majority of the citizens are ignorant about their rights and responsibilities. Those who are in positions of leadership seem to benefit so much from this ignorance that they would rather keep the status quo. They keep enforcing practices that keep the masses from this knowledge. They do this through controlling the media, removing the freedom of the press, killing or threatening journalists and silencing any voices of dissent. Meanwhile, they make deals with companies from within and outside our continent, which disadvantage the rightful owners of the resources, the citizens.

Dear young African citizen, you must learn to see this enemy that comes in different ways and shows up with different heads. One head that shows up frequently in our continent is corruption. It is such a silent robber, but is effectively taking away our birth right, right beneath our noses.

The Power Of Service

An argument arose among the twelve followers of a famous teacher. They wanted to know who would be the greatest among them. Who would the teacher value the most and what it would take for any of them to become the greatest among the twelve followers? There is no doubt that each of them had that desire to become the great one. Some were thinking that the teacher saw much value in them more than any other. The others thought the teacher was friendlier to them than to the rest of the team. When the famous teacher found out about the arguments in their hearts, he saw an opportunity to teach them about how each of them could multiply their value and become great, and this is what he said to them.

" .... whoever wants to become great among you must be your servant, and whoever wants to be first among you must be your slave."

That was a revolutionary statement, one that would be used to teach billions of people about leadership across the world. Jesus said this statement to His disciples. There are a few things that we want to unpack out of this statement as it applies to our lives and in the marketplace.

The word servant, in its literal sense, means a person who performs duties for others, especially a person employed in a house on domestic duties or as a personal attendant. The word slave means (especially in the past) a person who is the legal property of another and is forced to obey them. I am sure that when the disciples heard this, they must have thought that Jesus was confused. In those days, kings and queens used to rule over the people. They ruled over empires, and everyone in their territory or empire was under the *rulership* of that kingdom. Taxes and royalties were paid to the king to maintain the palace and enrich the king's household. Holding on to power was the order of the day.

If you were to ask any ordinary person on that day about what it took to become great among all people, they would have told you that you needed to have been born into a royal family. Some would have said you needed to have achieved massive success as a fighter in the army so that you overthrow the current king. Jesus introduced something new when He mentioned that the great people of the future would not be the rulers but would be the servants and slaves.

Let us take this into the marketplace and see how it applies in today's world. How do people become the richest in the world? The top 100 wealthiest people in the world are people who own businesses that 'serve' the needs of their customers. They are the people who would have forgotten all else and devoted themselves to the service of others through pursuing entrepreneurship.

Becoming an entrepreneur is an act of great self-sacrifice and courage for a higher value. No matter where you go in business, business leaders will tell you that the customer is king. The customer dictates where the products are going and what changes are needed on the product. The company that can produce the product or service that best solves the problem of the customer is the one that succeeds. Also, the more customers they reach with their solutions (products/services), the more money they make and the greater they become.

We can even take this to the world of politics. Gone are the days where people follow anyone who does not solve their problems but wants to serve their personal interests. The most successful leaders are those who have taken time to understand the needs of their electorate and have proposed solutions that work for their people. Those who try to cheat people to get power live in so much fear, as that kind of leadership is no longer sustainable. It is those leaders who demonstrate that they value people and will do everything in their power to serve, who succeed in leadership anywhere in the world.

Would you like to multiply your value? Do not waste time. Find a way that we can serve others. Let's find the best systems, processes, and resources to solve a particular problem that we see in our society. The more we do that, the better value we will create for ourselves. When we do that, people will hunt for us and give us their resources for us to continue the great work of service.

Serving others goes beyond the product or service that we produce to make a profit. It can have no profit in monetary terms at all, but it brings some intangible benefits. I love one of the statements on the JCI Creed, which says, "Service to humanity is the best work of life."

Not only do we get a sense of fulfilment when we serve others, but we also find our true purpose in life when we do so. Mahatma Gandhi, the great revolutionary Indian leader made this observation and said, "The best way to find yourself is to lose yourself in the service of others." When we devote ourselves to meeting other people's needs, and forget about our needs as we serve, there is a guarantee that we find what we are about as individuals.

I discovered my passion for social entrepreneurship and social innovation as I was serving in JCI as a project member. I found joy in helping others succeed and escape poverty. Up to now, my whole life is centred around helping people to lift themselves from where they are to a better place in one way or another. I focus on studying, practising, and teaching success principles primarily because I found that passion as I served. What are you doing to serve your community? Do you see something that needs fixing in your area? There is a reason why you see that problem, and there is a reason why it is bothering you so much. You were meant to solve that problem. As you try to find solutions to that challenge, chances are, you will find yourself too. This is precisely what Zig Ziglar, the great motivational speaker observed when he said, "You will get all you want in life if you help enough other people get what they want."

Developing Your Service Model –Choosing Your Playing Field

In the previous principle, we saw how important it is to serve others to multiply our value. The more people we serve, the more our value increases. The better quality of service, the more people will look for what we have to offer. In this chapter, I want to explain how one can develop a way to serve others in a way that multiplies your value in the quickest way possible and in a way that keeps the service going for a long time. The people that have mastered how to serve others in the most significant and most efficient ways have built products, people and processes that enable that to happen, and we have to learn from them so that we too, can see how to take what we have and serve the world.

First, let us talk about the number of ways that you can serve others in your chosen field. Three broad sectors exist where you can serve. These are the **private sector**, **public sector,** and **civil society**. The private sector is part of the economy that is not under direct state control. This sector usually comprises organisations run by individuals and groups who seek to generate and return a profit to owners. You find businessmen and businesswomen in this sector. At the highest level of serving in this sector, you find big companies owned by a few individuals or owned by many people and institutions through the stock exchange (Listed companies).

The great thing about developing yourself in this sector is that when you build and own a company, you serve in many ways by employing many people, contributing to the growth of the economy and you create wealth for yourself in the process. This is where the biggest philanthropists (those who promote the welfare of others, primarily through financial donations) are made. The multiplication of your value in this sector is directly related to how innovative, relevant, and efficient your solution is to the world. Most of the best products and services that we enjoy come from this sector - our phones, cars, the internet, food, entertainment, housing, and the list is endless. Even as an employee in this sector, you can be rewarded at a remarkably high level that allows you to grow and provide for your family.

It is an extremely competitive sector, and therefore you have to keep your eyes on the ball to ensure that the solution you are providing is leading, otherwise, if some other company can do a better job in providing that solution, you run out of business. This sector is also profit-driven. Profit is the way that you keep yourself in the game of serving. Otherwise, you have to close shop. So it has its limits because of the need to sustain itself through profits.

The public sector is part of the economy controlled by the state. This includes the provision of public goods and governmental services such as the military, police, infrastructure, public transport, public education, health care, and so on. This is where you find politicians (councillors, members of parliament, senators, cabinet ministers, governors and presidents) and other public servants who serve in different levels of government to meet the needs of the people.

Political parties are also part of this sector, and they play a vital role in directing how these public services are rendered to the public. If you want to measure the level of development of a country, one of the big things to look at is how the poor people are served when it comes to healthcare and education. You look at the quality of the infrastructure maintenance on things like roads, street lighting and the provision of services like electricity and education across that country. Like the private sector, some models are used to ensure that the best service is given to multiply your value in this sector. The great thing about serving in this sector is that you are involved in providing solutions that affect the lives of ordinary citizens and thus, you have an opportunity to improve their quality of life. I like what Moeletsi Mbeki says in his book, **'Advocates for Change'**.

He says, *"... it is the dominant political elite in any given society that determines whether a country develops or does not develop. Entrepreneurs of all descriptions – from pirates to inventors to investment bankers –play a critical role in the economic development process, but they can only do so if the dominant political elite allows them to play that role."*

In other words, this sector has the power to develop a nation or keep it stagnant. We urgently need a good crop of leading change-makers in this sector on our continent, Africa. Those who have the heart to serve for the greater good, even though their financial return may be low; value in this sector is not just measured in how wealthy you have become, but in how wealthy your country as a whole has become, and how the standard of living of your community has improved because of your influence, dear young African child. If you feel a burden for this area, do not look at what is and be discouraged. Look at what could be and be involved. We have a billion people to take care of, and you need to play a role in making that happen. They deserve nothing but the best.

The civil society consists of groups or organisations working in the interest of the citizens but operating outside of the government (public) and for-profit (private) sectors. Examples could include academia, activist groups, charities, clubs, community foundations, churches, and cooperatives. Some of the most renowned change-makers who fought for the recognition of human rights came from this sector. The names of people like Martin Luther King Jnr, and Archbishop Desmond Tutu come to mind. Most non-profit organisations fall under this category. Organisations like Transparency International, Care International, Wikimedia Foundation, Cure Violence, and Ceres are examples of top global non-governmental organisations (NGOs) that take care of people's different needs. Some focus on providing access to education, healthcare, the wellbeing of refugees, the upkeep of the environment and the list goes on.

In this sector, the big words that express value are Impact, Innovation, and Sustainability. Impact is the biggest measure of value in this area. Have the people's lives been improved because of this intervention? Has the government conduct or repressive laws been changed because of civil society intervention? Innovation speaks to finding new ways to meet these basic needs. Sustainability speaks to how long this impact will stay on in the people's lives. The best positive change is more permanent and lasting.

Once again, Africa needs strong civil society actors who can create positive change in our communities. One of the biggest challenges we have as society is how disengaged our citizens are when it comes to exercising their democratic rights and holding government to account. Government will only act as far as the citizens demand or expect. If the expectations are too low or there are none at all, politicians can get away with providing campaign T-shirts or a bag of maize meal to our citizens in exchange for a vote.

Great civil society actors will help bring this consciousness to the general population. Another challenge is over-dependency, where we have always relied on a third party to solve our problems. A civil society movement that enables our people to take responsibility for their future will go a long way in increasing our productivity as a continent, and thus will make us multiply our value.

Whatever it is you want to serve the people with will fit in somewhere within these three sectors. As a change maker, you must choose the playing field that best suits your SHAPE or that best expresses the solution you want to provide. Also, it is essential to know that you can serve in all three sectors, depending on what you are doing, but you need to choose a vehicle that best suits the terrain that you will travel in. A lot is known about how to serve in the private sector, and a lot has been said on how to develop your entrepreneurship habits in this book. I want to shed more light about how we can add value in the civic sector and the public sector as citizens who want to multiply our value.

The Political Service Model

Politics is a subject from which many people want to shy away. In most places, leaders in politics are seen as ruthless, lying, and cheating people because of promises they continuously make and do not deliver. The news headlines are usually filled with scandals about people involved in politics because that is where the media's attention is generally concentrated.

I remember when I was growing up, my mother would ask me what I wanted to do when I grow up. Naturally, one of the things I would say was that I wanted to be a president or a government minister because I just thought they had all the attention, the money, and they could change people's lives. My mother, being fully aware of the political environment in Zimbabwe, would say, "That's great Dr U. But maybe you should consider the kind of political leader who does not go out campaigning but one who is appointed for his technical knowledge, like a Health minister for example."

I could sense her fears of the political playing field and what it is known for. Many people in my country also grew up in the same way. Many options were considered to be alright as career paths, but when it came to politics, there was a sense of caution and fear.   Ultimately, other career paths are preferred, and the political one either comes as an after-thought or as a retirement option.

When I started High School in 1998, I began noticing the standard of life in my country changing. Certain political decisions were made, and we all heard about them but did not know the impact such decisions would have on our lives. By the year 2008, I fully understood the importance of politics in everyone's life. The political environment was unstable; inflation was at a historical record high and shops were empty. Savings in people's accounts and pensions were lost because of the political environment. As a young man studying business management, our lecturers used to tell us how the political environment would affect business, and my Zimbabwean experience gave me a real-life example of how that would come about. My interest in studying the impact of politics on the economy and the general wellbeing of the people grew as I started studying how economies work and why some countries, (especially African countries) were not doing well in these areas. I assumed that our nations are poor because we are not as hard-working or industrious as other countries are. We do not set high goals for ourselves, or we do not plan as much as other nations do. These were all assumptions in my head. As I travelled around the world and met with different people in different countries, I started gaining respect for the African people's sense of hard work. I started discovering that we were in these circumstances mostly because of our politics.

One of the books I recommend highly is a book called '**Why Nations Fail'** by Daron Acemoglu and James A Robinson. The two researchers studied how prosperous nations have developed and why certain countries were locked in a cycle of poverty. Surprisingly, the underlying causes of prosperity or failure were not in race, religion, culture, geography or even how educated the political leaders are. The major reason was about how the economic institutions of the country were run. The very root cause of how these economic institutions were run was with politics. Politics determine the institutions that a country has. Yes, colonialism was a political invasion of independent political institutions that also caused the perpetual impoverishment of many countries in the world. However, even after that era, many independent countries kept using the same methods used by colonial powers to govern their countries, and that is what has kept the countries impoverished.

In summary, the book explains how inclusive political institutions thrive over exclusive or extractive political institutions. It argues that inclusive institutions give birth to inclusive economic institutions where everyone has a fair shot at life and can prosper because of their great entrepreneurship abilities or because of their hard work. Extractive political institutions on the other hand, give birth to extractive (exclusive) economic institutions where a few people benefit from the economy while the rest of the people are suffering. In fact, the more the majority suffers, the better the few elite, politically powerful or connected people become. As I read through the history of many nations in the world, I could see how prosperous countries had evolved from extractive politics to inclusive politics, and why they started achieving this prosperity. I could also see why most of Africa is where it is right now, and my experience of living in different countries has shown me how this can directly affect the general population.

It is therefore essential that we address the issue of political institutions, political governance, and political leadership in our continent. We can only ignore this at our peril. If the 1.2 billion people on our continent are to have a great chance at life, where they receive proper health care, where almost all our people are gainfully employed and where they can live a longer life, we have to address the issue of political leadership. This is not as easy as just changing the individuals that lead our countries, but changing how our countries are led. Are we being led in a way that considers all people, where all people are equal, and their views and opinions can be equally expressed? Or are we being led in a way that only the connected and powerful can gain while others suffer? If we are being led in a way where the majority suffers, we need to find a way to start changing how we as citizens of this great continent are led. Here are a few suggestions on how we can get that to happen. Let me speak to our future politicians now. This is where we need to take our continent.

1. The thriving political leader of the future will have a heart of service. My dear leaders, we need to know that the positions of political leadership are not meant for us to become wealthy. They are opportunities for us to serve our countries and make life better for our generation and future generations. Let's change the way we see politics. Our current crop of leaders have taken the people for granted and have been tempted by the bribes and corruption that will keep eroding our wealth if we continue on that path.

2. The thriving political reformer of a prosperous Africa will have political intelligence. By this, I mean that

they will know how to study power and use their knowledge of power to empower the majority of the people. Nelson Mandela had an opportunity to become a billionaire when he became the president of South Africa, but he restrained himself and thought of the millions of people he was leading. Instead, he went on a mission to build thriving institutions that would make the government accountable, even after his time of service. He worked hard to get the freedom of the black majority of South Africa, but after attaining the freedom, he had the wisdom of knowing how to secure it. He gave the power back to the people through the creation of a powerful constitution, and by empowering the people to take a stand against bad leadership. It took courage for a political leader of a powerful party to say, "If the ANC does to you what the Apartheid government did to you, then you must do to the ANC what you did to the Apartheid government."

3. The future political leaders of a thriving continent will think more in terms of institutions than they think about individuals. Seretse Khama of Botswana could have taken advantage of his people when he had the opportunity to lead, but he gave his people a voice by practising real democracy, which birthed a legacy of a prospering country. That is the kind of intelligence we need from our future political leaders.

4. The political leaders who will make our continent thrive will have a big sense of sacrifice. They will sacrifice the gains they could have received using their power. They will be less wealthy than the current crop of leaders, but they will make room for

their countries to be extremely wealthy instead. They will set a legacy for future generations. They will shun corruption in all its shapes and forms and do the right thing for their countries to prosper.

5. Lastly, they will fire themselves by empowering the masses with knowledge about their rights and responsibilities in the country. They will therefore not hold onto power and so they must not be attached to power. It is such a shame that we have presidents that hold on to power until they are no longer fit to function correctly in our continent. Some have to be kicked out because they are treating our independent democracies as their little kingdoms. The future leader needs to know that this is not the way to go if our countries are to prosper. They will empower the people to fire them if they cross the line of good governance, and they will be happy to leave.

Are you one of the political leaders we desperately need in our continent? If you are, then start working towards it now by being active in the political sphere. Join a political party or form one. We depend on you ascending the political ladder, so work hard and work smart until you are in an influential position to change the status quo. They will not go down without a fight, so brace yourself for battle. Choose your battles well, and remember to work with people and treat them right on your way up. Those people will be a shield for you when the powerful start coming after you. Above all else, put your trust and faith in God. He has created you for such a time as this. You would not be reading this if it wasn't meant for you. He will never leave you nor forsake you. Be the example of the good shepherd who will release his sheep to multiply their value in peace.

The Civic Service Path

The civic sector has produced some of the most highly regarded change-makers in the world. These are change-makers who are neither in government nor in the private sector. Their most significant driving force is a cause that would have moved their hearts to take action and make life better for humankind or the environment.

As a result, they find themselves leading purpose or cause-driven organisations, not primarily to make a profit, but to create the change they desire in a specific field. Sometimes the people that lead this change do not have much capital to create this positive change, and sometimes throwing money at the situation will not solve the problem. However, these individuals usually possess social capital, that unique ability to have other ordinary citizens support their cause and create a massive demand for that particular issue to be addressed.

On December 1, 1955, a black lady called Rosa Parks was arrested in the city of Montgomery, Alabama state, in the United States of America. Rosa Parks' crime was that she sat in a section of the Cleveland Avenue bus reserved for white people, and this was a crime under Alabama's Jim Crow laws. Rosa Parks knew these laws and could have chosen to obey the laws and avoid being arrested, but she had a deep-seated cause or burden for fair treatment and freedom for people of colour in the Southern parts of America.

At that time, she was a secretary of the Montgomery Chapter of the National Association for the Advancement of Coloured People (NAACP), which focused on changing institutions of oppression. So yes, when she sat there, she was conscious of what she was doing. She intended to challenge the system and decided to sit where she was not allowed in protest. Her arrest triggered several organised protests that lasted 17 days and led to changes in the laws that allowed for that segregation. The protests involved many, and among those who were the masterminds was Dr Martin Luther King Jnr.

Rosa Parks is an example of an influential leader in the civic society who sought change, acted upon the change she desired, and inspired many to join that cause and achieve freedom for many in society.

There are many lessons to learn from people like Rosa. Firstly, she was a member of an association in civic society that represented the things that she cared about. We do not hear that she was Founder of a multinational corporation or President of a church. She was serving in an association that promoted the cause of equality that she genuinely cared about. There is no doubt that while in this organisation, she met like-minded people who shared the same concerns she had.

Usually, organisations like these are voluntary. She probably had her full-time job, but in her spare time, she cared enough to be involved in a cause bigger than her. The same goes for Dr Martin Luther King Jnr, who was a full-time pastor. There is more that you can do to contribute to your society. Your job is for your survival and upkeep, but your job does not define you. You can do much more. What organisation are you a part of that represents the causes that you feel so strongly about? You do not have to join and lead, you can be a member, and you never know where that will take you. Rosa Parks, equipped with the philosophy of freedom and knowledge of her constitutional rights, and empowered by her constant association with like-minded people, overcame the fear of the police and repressive laws of her time. She decided to sit in her rightful place, and that bold act of hers stirred up a revolution. The revolution changed the lives of many.

I have been a member of Junior Chamber International for over ten years now, an organisation of young people that believe that we need to take responsibility for our development. As a member, I have learnt a lot of powerful lessons, just serving in projects. In 2012, when I was a local president of JCI City in Harare, Zimbabwe, we supported a youth development organisation called the Youth Empowerment Trust in Kuwadzana Township.

The members of JCI City devoted their time to teach life skills to the young people in the program every weekend. We taught them how to draft their CVs so that they could prepare for work, how to handle their hygiene and health, and how to develop their confidence. To us, these skills were simple, but to these young people, this was information they needed and one could tell from their reaction and responses to us. We had medical doctors, accountants, lawyers, artists, and scientists in our team, and we all shared our time with them. I will never forget the look in one of the founder's eyes when I brought five computers to their offices for the youth to learn computer skills. My employer had donated these old computers, which were lying idle in the offices. For the organisation, they rejoiced as if they were receiving brand new computers. Until today, I still keep in touch with the organisation. We made a contribution that transformed other people's lives, and it did not take much from us.

In the same year, we supported an orphanage in Highfields township. We paid monthly visits, and when we realised that the pass rate for their O Level students (Matric) and Grade Seven students were going down, we decided to offer free lessons to them. That year, all the students who were writing exams passed. Some students just needed a little bit of encouragement and some only needed simple things like a calculator to use in a review and when we could easily provide these for them, they felt that they had bigger brothers and sisters who could support them. That made a significant impact on their lives.

What is it that you have in your hands? You have something. It could be your time, your love, resources, education, shelter, spiritual gifts and the list goes on. What can you do with what you have to help other people move ahead? If the task sounds too daunting and lonely, then ask yourself this question. What do I care about? Is it the spiritual nourishment of others? If so, then join an organisation that promotes that and give your time to teaching others in your spare time. Is it singing? Then why not join a choir that produces great music to help others relax and be entertained. You have so much to give, and there is a whole world in need of your help, so start doing something meaningful with it. Give yourself away.